THE WORSHIP HANDBOOK

DEVELOPING

THE HEART OF A WORSHIPER

IN YOUR MINISTRY TEAM

MARQUIS ASHLEY

The Worship Handbook
Copyright © 2026 Marquis Ashley
Published by: Steadfast Publishing

Cover design: Marquis Ashley
Printed in the United States of America
Scripture quotations are from:
NIV Bible © 1978, 1984, 2011 Biblica
NLT Bible © 1996 Tyndale
ESV Bible © 2001 Crossway
Used by permission. All rights reserved.

ISBN: 979-8-9941348-0-1

— . —

This book is dedicated to my family who has served faithfully in
church ministry alongside me through the years
with willing and generous hearts.

God loves a cheerful giver.

Thank you for the sacrifices you have made to serve
God, The Church, The Lost, The Team and The Moment.

As for me and my house, we will serve the Lord.

And to the amazing teams God has allowed me to pastor and
work with. You have been a joy and I'm so grateful for the ways
you have blessed and ministered to me over the years.

— . —

CONTENTS

PREFACE **7**

CHAPTER 1   **WE ARE ALL WORSHIPERS** **9**

CHAPTER 2   **WHO DO WE WORSHIP?** **23**

CHAPTER 3   **WHY DO WE WORSHIP?** **35**

CHAPTER 4   **WHAT IS WORSHIP?** **43**

CHAPTER 5   **HOW DO WE WORSHIP?** **53**

CHAPTER 6   **THE FIVE C's** **73**

CHAPTER 7   **THE FIVE P's** **85**

CHAPTER 8   **TEAM VALUES** **95**

CHAPTER 9   **MUSIC IN THE BIBLE** **105**

CHAPTER 10   **WORSHIP IN THE PRACTICAL** **133**

PREFACE

Dear Reader,

I wrote this book to be the kind of encouragement and resource I wish I would have had when I first began this journey of servant-leadership in worship and church ministry. I wanted to write something that was both easily accessible to adults and students alike and useful for both the individual's edification, as well as team training, reflection and discussion.

My hope is that this book becomes a tool for you whether you are a pastor, a church staff member, a volunteer, a worship leader, musician or creative. May it be a resource that challenges, equips, and strengthens you both spiritually and practically. I pray it helps you grow in your understanding of worship and prepares you for the work and lifestyle of worship that God has called you to.

What the world needs is not another prodigy performer, celebrity, or superstar. The world simply needs more true and humble worshipers—selfless servant-leaders who understand their desperate need for grace, who see the beauty of God's love and holiness, and who respond with lives surrendered to His leadership.

The heart of a worshiper is one that responds to the gospel with a life lived on mission for the glory of God. It's a heart and mind devoted to right thinking, right living, and the offering of every gift and skill for the Lord's use. More than anything, this world needs Jesus, and it needs to see genuine worshipers who live to know Him and to make Him known.

May this book help set that tone in your heart. May it spur you on toward love and good deeds, not to earn God's love or favor, but as a joyful response to the love and favor already shown to us through the cross. We love because He first loved us, and now we live our lives as worshipers, saying:

Thank You, Lord, for saving me and setting me free from sin, wrath, and death. You have purchased me out of the slave market of sin and made me a free person, a new creation in Christ. I will live my life with open hands and an open heart, ready for whatever You want *for* me and *from* me, because I know Your plans are better than my own. You are Savior and You are Lord. Lead me wherever You will. My life is Yours.

"Therefore, I urge you, brothers and sisters, to offer your bodies as a living sacrifice, holy and pleasing to God—this is your spiritual and reasonable act of worship."
—Romans 12:1

1

WE ARE ALL WORSHIPERS

We Are All Worshipers

Every human being on the planet is a worshiper. The question isn't *if* we worship, it's *who* or *what* we worship. Our worship flows from what we value most, and that depends on our worldview, beliefs, and the posture of our hearts, whether they're marked by pride or humility.

In much of today's world, and especially in the West, independence and self-reliance are celebrated. We're taught to chase after power, praise, position, possessions and comfort, but thinking and living with a self-indulgent focus is always idolatrous, and idolatry is spiritual adultery. These empty pursuits are the opposite of what God created us for, yet we sadly see them too often in the church and in the lives of believers, which begs the question: "Who or what are we truly worshiping?"

We were made to walk in an intimate relationship with the Maker of the universe, the Lover of our souls, who holds all wisdom, love, and life in His hands. Yet often we turn away from Him to chase after other lovers that can never satisfy.

When we worship anything other than God, we step into an identity we weren't created for and find only temporary pseudo fulfillment. That type of worship destroys the soul, and it's exactly what the Lord longs to save us from.

> *"They exchanged the truth of God for a lie, and worshiped and served created things rather than the Creator—who is forever praised. Amen."*
> *— Romans 1:25*

When we live for ourselves, we exchange the truth of God for a lie, we cripple our fruitfulness, and we rob God of the glory He deserves.

We are all worshipers, and in the end, every one of us will worship something. We can either worship ourselves as false gods or worship the one true God who alone is worthy.

The Root of All Sin Is Pride

At the root of every sin is pride, the belief that we know better than God. When we say, "I'll do it my way," we make ourselves our own gods, but in Christianity, there can be no idols, not even ourselves. Unfortunately, *we* are often our own biggest obstacle to spiritual growth.

One of the saddest stories in Scripture is the story of Cain and Abel. Only two generations into humanity after creation, we see one of the worst of evils happening, and between brothers!

Genesis 4, recounts the first murder—the jealousy-fueled killing of Abel by his brother, Cain. Abel had brought an acceptable offering to the Lord, while Cain's was rejected. God knew what was happening in Cain's heart and warned him, saying in Genesis 4:6-7:

> *Why are you angry? Why is your face downcast? If you do what is right, will you not be accepted? But if you do not do what is right, sin is crouching at your door; it desires to have you, but you must rule over it.*

Well, we all know what happens next. Cain *doesn't* rule over his emotions and sin, and ends up murdering his brother. God brings judgment upon Cain, and he's cast out to be a wanderer all his days.

When we're tempted to sin because of our pride, we must cry out to the Lord for help, and as God said, *master* sin. We must *rule over* the sinful inclinations and desires of our hearts!

God warned Cain in Genesis 4, "Sin is crouching at your door; it desires to have you, but you must rule over it." The same warning applies to us. Pride waits at the door, ready to deceive us into thinking we are the god of our own lives and can lead and govern ourselves how we want without consequences, but this shouldn't be the attitude of the believer.

Israel's history shows us what happens when pride and compromise enter worship. During the time of the kings, God's people mixed true worship with pagan practices. They offered sacrifices to the LORD, but also to their idols of sinful pleasure, comfort and convenience. Their hearts were divided. God continually called them back to Himself through the prophets, urging them to worship in spirit and truth, but most resisted and found nothing but pain and sorrow for it.

What You Worship Reveals Who You Are

Every person was designed to worship. The real question is: *what holds your heart?*

Isaiah declared in Isaiah 26:9:

*"At night **my soul longs for You**;*
*indeed, my spirit within me **seeks You** diligently."*

And David cried out in Psalm 63:1-7:

[1] God, you are my God,
   ***earnestly I seek you**;*
I thirst for you,
   ***my whole being longs for you**,*
in a dry and parched land
   where there is no water.
[2] I have seen you in the sanctuary
   and beheld your power and your glory.
*[3] Because **your love is better than life**,*
   my lips will glorify you.
[4] I will praise you as long as I live,
   and in your name I will lift up my hands.
[5] I will be fully satisfied as with the richest of foods;
   with singing lips my mouth will praise you.
[6] On my bed I remember you;
   ***I think of you** through the watches of the night.*
[7] Because you are my help,
   I sing in the shadow of your wings.

THIS is the heart of a worshiper—someone who *loves God* and has found their identity and treasure in *Him* alone.

When we compare ourselves with Isaiah and David, what is it that *we* think about when *we* lie awake at night? Is it:

- A new car?
- A new guitar?
- That girl or guy?
- Success, fame, or approval?

Whatever captivates our thoughts, motivates our actions, and governs our decisions—that is what we worship.

True life and fulfillment are only found in knowing and walking with our good and holy God. *This* is a lifestyle of *worship*.

Some Background

I grew up in Spokane, Washington watching MTV in the 90's, and playing video games and street hockey in suburban cul-de-sacs with my brothers. My parents both came from broken homes and difficult upbringings, but they were determined to provide a good home and raise their kids with a sense of right and wrong. We weren't a particularly religious family. My dad didn't attend church ever, and my mom only took my siblings and me to the Catholic church down the street on occasion when someone had a guilty conscience, or on Christmas or Easter.

Though I don't remember hearing the gospel clearly communicated at that time, one thing I took away from my experience that I still appreciate to this day, was the sense of *reverence*. God was unmistakably holy in that place, and that awareness of holiness—of treating God with respect and awe—stuck with me. If nothing else, I'm thankful for that.

Sadly, I think reverence is too often missing in today's churches. From time to time, the pendulum seems to swing from one extreme to another. Sometimes God is made out to be cold and unapproachable in His holiness. Other times, He is treated with little to no reverence or respect at all. I believe there's a healthy balance to be had of both the holiness and warmth of God. While we want people to know God's love, we must never forget that He is also holy and worthy of our deepest respect.

In the United States, our culture has changed drastically since the days when biblical truth and Judeo-Christian ethics were a shared foundation. We've gone from a society that generally valued moral standards and had a sense of shame over sin to one that celebrates self-expression and rejects absolute truth, but as followers of Christ, we are called to live differently—to be set apart and transformed by the renewing of our minds.

"Therefore, I urge you, brothers and sisters, to offer your bodies as a living sacrifice, holy and pleasing to God—this is

Search for Identity

When I was seventeen, I believed there was a God out there somewhere, but I didn't understand who Jesus was, what He had done, and that I could have a saving relationship with Him. I was lost and wandering, searching for meaning and identity in all the wrong places: music, relationships, rebellion and drugs. I was the kind of teenager most parents didn't want their kids hanging out with.

Then one day, God used a young man named Devin to forever change my life. Devin was a humble, clean-cut, kind and caring Christian kid who approached me at school, turned me on to some not-so-lame Christian music, and invited me to a high school guys' Bible study. I was intrigued, both by his kindness and by His relationship with God, so I went.

When I arrived, there were five or six high school guys, some host parents, and an adult leader there, who welcomed me, fed me good food (always a plus), and gave me a Bible. They didn't judge me. They weren't afraid of my sin, my appearance or my rebellion. They just loved me and began to disciple me, and that love, along with the truth of God's Word, changed everything.

During that season, I was also invited to a Christian concert where I heard the gospel clearly proclaimed for the first time.

That night, in a crowded arena, I found myself alone in the presence of God. I knew that I was a sinner in need of a Savior, and when I heard that Jesus, God in flesh, took my punishment on the cross for my sin and was raised from the dead on the third day so I could have forgiveness and eternal life, I responded, surrendering my life to Him in faith and repentance.

From that night on, God began to transform my heart. He gave me new desires, new direction, and a passion to respond to His love by serving Him with my life and gifts. He even transformed my family; my parents and siblings came to Christ soon after as well.

So, dare to be a *Devin*. Reach out to the lost, the overlooked, the ones searching for meaning. You never know how many lives might be changed because you did.

The Gospel Changes Everything

When I put my trust in Christ, everything shifted. My music, my goals, my identity—everything that once revolved around *me* now revolved around *Him*. Life was no longer about *my* pleasure or worldly success; it was about *His* glory; and music became more than self-expression or a way to get money, girls, and popularity. It became an instrument of worship—a way to pray, to praise, to learn, to teach, and to serve others. Music became a way to grow closer to God and a way to reach people with His truth and love.

After high school, I told my parents I wanted to go to Bible College, to which my dad responded with roaring laughter saying, *"WHY? Do you want to be a PASTOR or something?"*

I clearly felt the disdain and mockery.

But after seeing God's work in my heart and the changes in me, he started attending my church and his heart began to soften. Before long, God gave me the courage to share the gospel with him, and at the age of fifty-two, he surrendered his life to Christ. In just a few short years God transformed not just my dad and I, but my whole family, and I am forever grateful.

"I am not ashamed of the gospel, for it is the power of God

for salvation to everyone who believes."

—Romans 1:16

God's grace took a rebellious, self-centered teenager along with his family and saved them, transformed them, and made them disciple-makers, missionaries, worshipers, and witnesses of His goodness, love and power. That's what the gospel does— *it changes everything!*

Don't Follow Your Dreams

"For Christ's love compels us...

that those who live should no longer live for themselves,

but for Him who died for them and was raised again."

—2 Corinthians 5:14–15

In my young adult years, my band was signed to an independent record label and then to a major label (back when those were still a thing). First, we began touring the west coast and then nationally, with a few international trips mixed in. It was an exciting time. I loved writing and recording and making great music with really talented friends, and pointing people to Jesus through it, but a few years in God spoke to my heart and called me out of the performance life, not because it was a bad or sinful vocation, but because He had something else for me.

I wrestled with it for a few months because I didn't want to let go of *my* "dream" for *my* gift and *my* music, but God lovingly reminded me that I was called to follow *Him* and *His* loving leadership in my life—and that ultimately, my life and talents were a gift from *Him* and *He* was to be the center of my life and worship, not *me* and *my* ambitions.

He spoke to my heart during that time and said:

*"Marquis, following Me isn't about you doing what **you** want to do for Me. It's about you doing what **I** want you to do for Me."*

Following Jesus isn't about us

doing what WE want to do for Him,

it's about us doing what HE wants

us to do for Him.

It was a pretty obvious truth, but one I needed to hear nonetheless, and that truth changed everything for me.

I can probably count on one hand the amount of times God has spoken that clearly to my heart. It was one of those moments where His voice almost seemed audible. It was powerful and it gave me great confidence to take the next step forward, to trust Him and to *stay the course* when difficulties arose in the season of life and ministry that was to follow.

When I let go of what I thought I wanted in order to embrace God's desires for me, I learned that God's plans for my life were far better than my own.

They tell me to abandon You to make my dreams come true,
but what am I supposed to do if I only dream of You?
—John Ellis

The world often tells us to "follow your dreams", but as believers, we need to make sure that Christ is our focus and that we're taking our cues from Him. He alone is the Way, the Truth and the Life. We aren't called to "follow our own hearts", "chase our dreams" or "find ourselves" by exploiting others or exploring all our own imaginations, desires and selfish ambitions. We aren't meant to build our own empires and kingdoms here on the earth. We were meant for more—something eternal.

Jesus said to seek first *His* kingdom and *His* righteousness (Matthew 6:33). He said we must *deny ourselves*, take up our cross, and *follow Him* (Matthew 16:24). He told us if we cling to our life we will lose it; but if we *give up our lives* for Him, we will find them. (Matthew 10:39)

On one hand He calls us to *die to self* and yet on the other, He tells us we will find *true rest* for our souls and *life abundant* when we trust and walk with Him in humble and loving surrender and obedience. It almost seems contradictory, yet somehow in this dichotomy we find the heart of a worshiper and the fullness of life that we were created for.

As I took those early steps of obedience in my young adult years—surrendering my dreams for music, like Abraham surrendering his promised future in Isaac, in Genesis 22, God was faithful and blessed me with more than I could have ever imagined. I sensed His presence and pleasure as He built my character and led me into greater joy and fruitfulness in ministry than ever before. Now, after 25 years in church ministry, from janitorial to tech, students, missions, worship, church-planting, and pastoring, I can say His ways are far better than mine. It's not always *comfortable*. It rarely means having the *applause of men* or enjoying *upward mobility*, but it's incredibly fulfilling to walk in God's plans for us and see the spiritual fruit that it produces. As my good friend Greg would say, *"It's not always easy to follow Jesus, but it's always worth it."*

"Delight yourself in the Lord, and He will give you the desires of your heart."
—Psalm 37:4

When our relationship with the Lord is in its proper place, our hearts align with His and *His* dreams become *our* dreams.

When we surrender our ambitions to Him and submit ourselves to *His* loving leadership—when we watch people being brought from death to life in Christ and know that we are playing a part in loving, equipping, and discipling them— we are filled with an indescribable sense of peace, pleasure, power, and purpose, and our heart's greatest desire becomes to fulfill *God's dreams*, build *His kingdom*, and walk in *His good plans* for our lives.

"For we are God's handiwork, created in Christ Jesus

to do good works, which God prepared in advance for us to do."

—Ephesians 2:10

Every person on the planet is a worshiper, so let's set our hearts on the only One who is truly worthy and worship Him.

Reflection & Discussion Questions

1. When you think back on your own story, where do you see God's hand guiding and redeeming your past?
2. How have pride or misplaced worship affected your walk with God?
3. Who was a "Devin" in your life and how can you be one for someone else?
4. What has God asked you to surrender so He can use you more fully (a dream, an idol, an attitude, etc.)?
5. How does the gospel reshape your identity and purpose as a worshiper?

2

WHO DO WE WORSHIP?

The Object of Our Worship

Every act of worship has an object.

Every song, prayer, or moment of adoration is directed *toward someone or something.*

As we established in chapter one, the question is never *"Do we worship?"* but *"Who, or what, are we worshiping?"*

In a culture filled with distractions, temptations and competing voices, the answer to that question shapes everything about our lives and ministries. If the object of our worship is wrong, then everything else—our work, our relationships, our music, our service, even our motives will be off-center, but when the object of our worship is rightly fixed on the Lord, everything else comes into alignment.

Jesus said in **John 4:23–24**:

"A time is coming and has now come when the true worshipers will worship the Father in spirit and in truth, for they are the kind of worshipers the Father seeks. God is spirit, and His worshipers must worship in spirit and in truth."

True worship begins with an accurate view of *who* God is.

So who is God?

The Trinity

God has revealed Himself as triune, and the three Persons of the Godhead share the same nature and essence. Each has all the qualities of divinity and is eternal and unchanging. The Father is God (John 6:27, Romans 1:7, 1 Peter 1:2). The Son is God (John 1:1-14, Romans 9:5, Colossians 2:9, Hebrews 1:8, 1 John 5:20). The Holy Spirit is God (Acts 5:3-4, 1 Corinthians 3:16), but there is only *one* God. That is the biblical doctrine of the Trinity.

The One True God

Deuteronomy 6:4 declares, "Hear, O Israel: The Lord our God, the Lord is one." This foundational monotheistic verse emphasizes God's unique, singular nature, instructing Israel and all believers to worship Him exclusively and to love Him completely, a concept echoed in the New Testament by Jesus and the apostles (Mark 12:29, 1 Corinthians 8:4, 1 Timothy 2:5).

Though we worship a triune Godhead who has revealed himself as Father, Son and Holy Spirit, He has made it unmistakably clear that He is *One* and that He alone is worthy of worship.

He declares in **Isaiah 45:5**:

> *"I am the LORD, and there is no other;*
> *apart from Me there is no God."*

All other so-called gods are false—idols of man's imagination and invention. The God of the Bible is not just one deity among many; He is the Creator, the Sustainer, the Redeemer, and the Righteous Judge of all.

He is:

Holy—completely set apart from sin and imperfection (Isaiah 6:3)

Loving—full of mercy and steadfast kindness (Exodus 34:6)

Faithful—unchanging in His promises (Lamentations 3:22–23)

Sovereign—is the ultimate judge and authority over all creation (Acts 17:24-25)

When we begin to grasp even a glimpse of His greatness, our worship becomes more than a song. It becomes a response of reverence, awe, and gratitude.

God The Father

Many people unfortunately have less than ideal, and even terrible, earthly fathers, so it can be hard for some to imagine or celebrate the fact that our Creator God desires for us to view Him as such. For those of us with good earthly fathers, we can easily grasp the idea of a loving God who desires what's best for us, and approach Him with a healthy childlike dependence.

Whether you've had the ideal father or a poor representation of what fatherhood should look like, I hope that you can recognize the truth of God's eternal, holy and loving nature as the perfect Father. He is Love (1 John 4:8). He holds us and strengthens us (Isaiah 41:10). He fights for us (Exodus 14:14). He is patient and slow to anger (Psalm 145:8, 2 Peter 3:9). He listens to us and cares for us (Psalm 116:1-2, 1 Peter 5:7). He holds all wisdom and desires to give it to us (James 1:5). He wants to protect us from the negative effects of sin and He even disciplines us, as a loving Father should, to save us from future danger and destruction (Heb 12:5-11).

To be loved by God as a Father, means we are:

- **Adopted** (Romans 8:15, Ephesians 1:5, Galatians 4:4-7)
- **Beloved** (Ephesians 5:1, Colossians 3:12, 1 Thessalonians 1:4)
- **Children** (John 1:12, Ephesians 5:1, 1John 3:1)
- **Heirs** (Romans 8:17, Galatians 4:7, Titus 3:7)

How amazing it is that we have a God who exists as, and declares Himself to be, our Father.

God The Holy Spirit

In addition to The Father, God exists *as* and has revealed Himself to us *in* the Person of The Holy Spirit. The Holy Spirit is not merely a force or energy, like in Star Wars, that we conjure or learn to use for our supernatural advantage. The Holy Spirit is not a *thing* or an *it*, but a *He*. He is God.

As God, He *convicts* the world of sin, righteousness, and judgement (John 16:8). He *guides* us into truth (John 16:13). He *testifies* of and brings glory to Christ (John 15:26, 16:14). His indwelling presence marks each believer when we come to faith in Christ. He is the *seal* and *deposit* guaranteeing our inheritance (Eph 1:13-14).

Our bodies are the *temple* of the Holy Spirit (1 Corinthians, 6:19) and we can *resist* Him (Acts 7:51), *quench* Him (1 Thessalonians 5:19), and *grieve* Him (Ephesians 4:30) by walking according to the flesh, or we can live a life that is full and pleasing to God, by walking *in the Spirit* (Galatians 5:16-25). He is our *Counselor, Helper* and *Comforter* (John 14:16, 14:26, 15:26). He *gives us spiritual gifts* (Romans 12, 1 Corinthians 12, Ephesians 4). He *enables* us to live spiritually fruitful lives (Galatians 5:22) and *empowers* us for bold and effective ministry (Acts 1:8, 4:8, 4:31).

When we are led by the Holy Spirit, we will live godly lifestyles and use His generous giftings to lead people into truth by edifying other believers and pointing the lost to Christ who is their only hope of salvation. When His gifts are used correctly, God is glorified and worshiped rather than an individual, group or organization.

What a gift to have the Presence of God indwelling us to sanctify us, strengthen us, and help us to live holy and healthy lives! Let's walk in the Spirit and make our lives count for the glory of God and the salvation of souls. Amen?

And without further ado...

God The Son

One of the best ways to learn about the character and nature of God is by looking at the life and ministry of Jesus, God incarnate. He is not simply a moral teacher, prophet, or historical figure. He is *Immanuel*, God with us (Isaiah 7:14, Matthew 1:23).

The Word Made Flesh

"In the beginning was the Word, and the Word was with God, and the Word was God... Through Him all things were made."
—John 1:1-3

The Greek word for "Word" in this famous passage is **Logos**. Jesus is the eternal Logos—the very *expression* of God's heart, mind, and will.

"The Word became flesh and made His dwelling among us."
—John 1:14

God's divine nature was revealed in human form as He walked among His creation.

The Exact Representation of God

Jesus isn't similar to God, resembling God, made up of the same stuff as God, nor was He created by God; Jesus *is* the clear manifestation of *God in flesh*.

"He is the image of the invisible God...
by Him all things were created, in heaven and on earth."
—Colossians 1:15-16

"In Him all the fullness of Deity dwells in bodily form."
—Colossians 2:9

"The Son is the radiance of God's glory
and the exact imprint of His nature."
—Hebrews 1:3

**Jesus didn't just reflect God—He *revealed* Him.
He *is* God.**

Jesus said, *"I and the Father are one"* (John 10:30) and, *"Anyone who has seen Me has seen the Father"* (John 14:6–7).

The "I Am" of Scripture

Jesus' identity is not hidden. It is declared openly throughout the Gospels. Through seven "I Am" statements, He reveals Himself as the source and sustainer of all life:

1. ***"I am the Bread of Life"***—our spiritual sustenance (John 6)

2. ***"I am the Light of the World"***—our illumination in darkness (John 8)

3. ***"I am the Door"***—our access to salvation (John 10)

4. ***"I am the Good Shepherd"***—our protector and guide (John 10)

5. ***"I am the Resurrection and the Life"***—our hope beyond the grave (John 11)

6. ***"I am the Way, the Truth, and the Life"***—our only path to the Father (John 14)

7. ***"I am the True Vine"***—our source of fruitfulness and connection (John 15)

Beyond these, Jesus boldly proclaimed His eternal existence when He said, *"Before Abraham was, I Am"* (John 8:58). In response to His statement, the crowd picked up stones to stone Him as a blasphemer. They understood *exactly* what He was claiming—He was claiming to be *God* by identifying Himself with the eternal "*I Am*" of Exodus 3:14.

Then at His arrest in *John 18*, when Jesus declared, "*I Am,*" the mob fell backward to the ground, showing that He had power over them and that His surrender was voluntary, not forced. Jesus is *The Great I Am!*

The Exalted Christ

At the end of the story, we see Jesus not just as the suffering servant, but as the triumphant King.

Revelation 19:11–16 paints the awe-inspiring scene:

"Then I saw heaven opened, and behold, a white horse! The one sitting on it is called Faithful and True, and in righteousness He judges and makes war. His eyes are like a flame of fire, and on His head are many crowns... His name is called The Word of God... and on His robe and on His thigh, He has a name written:
King of kings and Lord of lords."

He is the Alpha and the Omega, the Beginning and the End (Revelation 22:13). He is both the Root and the Offspring of David, the promised Messiah (Revelation 22:16). He is the unchanging One who is the same yesterday, today, and forever (Hebrews 13:8).

This is the Jesus we worship—eternal, uncreated, holy and victorious.

The Deity of Christ: The Only Option

Humanity has tried to reduce Jesus into manageable categories:

- The Jews see Him as a mere rabbi
- Muslims call Him a prophet
- Mormons believe He was a man who became a god
- Hindus add Him as one of many gods
- Jehovah's Witnesses claim He is a lesser, angelic being

But Jesus and His disciples never left those options open to us. The Bible is *clear*—He is not simply a teacher or prophet, nor is He merely a created being. He is *THE* Creator and Sustainer of all.

C.S. Lewis put it perfectly in *Mere Christianity when he said*:

"I am trying here to prevent anyone saying the really foolish thing that people often say about Him: 'I'm ready to accept Jesus as a great moral teacher, but I don't accept his claim to be God'. That is the one thing we must not say. A man who was merely a man and said the sort of things Jesus said would not be a great moral teacher. He would either be a lunatic—on the level with the man who says he is a poached egg—or else he would be the Devil of Hell. You must make your choice. Either this man was, and is, the Son of God, or else a madman or something worse. You can shut him up for a fool, you can spit at him and kill him as a demon or you can fall at his feet and call him Lord and God, but let us not come with any patronizing nonsense about his being a great human teacher. He has not left that open to us. He did not intend to."

There is no middle ground. He is Lord of all or He is nothing.

The Rejected King

When Jesus entered Jerusalem on Palm Sunday, crowds shouted, *"Hosanna! Blessed is He who comes in the name of the Lord!"* Yet within days, many of those same voices cried, *"Crucify Him!"*

The crowd's expectations of a political Messiah who would overthrow Roman rule were shattered when Jesus presented Himself as a humble king focused on spiritual salvation. Just like them, the world we live in today is so often concerned with external success at the expense of their spiritual condition and eternal end-state. This is what breaks the heart of God.

Luke records that as Jesus approached the city,

"He wept over it, saying, 'If you had only known on this day what would bring you peace... but you did not recognize the time of God's coming to you.'"
—Luke 19:41–44

And again, in Matthew's gospel, Jesus lamented:

"O Jerusalem, Jerusalem... How often I have longed to gather your children together as a hen gathers her chicks under her wings, but you were not willing."
—Matthew 23:37

The tragedy of human history is that many recognize Jesus' name and know He holds something of value, yet refuse to admit their need and allow His loving lordship in their lives.

Yet to those who do receive Him, He offers salvation and new life:

The Worshiper's Response

So who do we worship?

We worship a triune God who has revealed Himself to us as God The Father, God The Son, and God The Holy Spirit. He is Holy and He is Love.

He speaks of us in the most intimate and endearing terms, calling us: *adopted, beloved, children*, and *heirs*. He even refers to us, the church, as the *bride* of Christ (2 Corinthians 11:2, Revelation 19:7, Revelation 21:9). These are all extremely descriptive, meaningful, relational designations that reveal the incredible value our God places on us, and the desire He has for us to be near Him.

We worship a good Father, a sanctifying and empowering Holy Spirit, and we worship Jesus Christ, the eternal Son of God— the Word made flesh, the Lamb who was slain, the Risen King, who is the now and future Lord of glory who will reign forevermore.

He is faithful, trustworthy, and true. He is the same yesterday, today, and forever, and because of His nature and character our worship is not merely emotion, music, preference or performance. It is a response to seeing who God is and surrendering to His greatness.

When we see the Lord rightly, we respond rightly. When we behold His glory, we can't help but bow in humility, saying with the saints and angels:

> "Worthy is the Lamb who was slain,
> to receive power and wealth and wisdom and strength
> and honor and glory and praise!"
> —*Revelation 5:12*

Who we worship, and our recognition of His worth, is the heartbeat of our worship.

Reflection & Discussion Questions

1. How would you describe who God is in your own words?
2. What does it mean to you to be loved by God as a Father?
3. Which attribute of Christ most deeply shapes your worship?
4. After considering the person and work of the Holy Spirit, what do you think it should look like to be led by Him in life and ministry?
5. What are some ways your worship team can better ensure that every lyric, prayer, and action, reflects and honors The Father, The Son, and The Holy Spirit?
6. When you consider Jesus' identity, humility, sacrifice, and victory, how should that change the way you approach worship?

3

WHY DO WE WORSHIP?

Our "Why"

Every believer and every worship team needs to know *why* we do what we do. Why do we gather each week to sing, serve, pray, and proclaim? Why do we give our time, energy, and creativity to ministry? Why as created beings do we even exist?

Our "why" is simple, yet profound:

We exist to GLORIFY and ENJOY God.

The Westminster Shorter Catechism declares this foundational truth, by asking the question of all questions:

"What is the chief end of man?"

It answers by giving a summary of biblical truth:

"Man's chief end is to glorify God and to enjoy Him forever."

That's the heart of worship. We were created *by* Him, *for* Him, and to live *unto* Him. We were created for a relationship with God, and we worship not only because it's our duty, but because it's our deepest delight and what we were ultimately made for.

Glorify and Enjoy Him

On one hand, it's our *duty* to bow before our Creator—the One who spoke the universe into being. He is holy, sovereign, and all-powerful. Even if He were an unkind being, He would still deserve our worship, because *He is God and we are not*. He is the Creator; we are His creation.

But praise God, He is not an unkind or selfish ruler. He is a good, loving, and just God, a benevolent King, and a faithful Father who loves us with a perfect and holy love. So we worship not merely out of *obligation*, but out of *adoration*. We glorify Him because He is worthy, and we enjoy Him because He is good.

The Lord delights in His people, and He invites us into relationship with Himself. Scripture says we can *please Him* (Hebrews 13:16), *bring Him joy* (Zephaniah 3:17), and even *grieve His Spirit* (Ephesians 4:30). He is not distant. He is near, inviting us to walk and talk with Him daily. What an amazing God. Though He dwells in brilliant unapproachable light and holiness (1 Timothy 6:16), He also desires and makes a way for us to walk in relationship with Him by imputing Christ's righteousness to us who have believed in His atoning work.

He is both *holy* AND *loving*, *transcendent* yet *intimate*, our "Abba Father" (Romans 8:15), or as they say in India, "Pita Ji" meaning "Daddy Sir". It captures the intimacy of perfect familial love while also maintaining the reverence and honor which are due to a father.

Just like a child, we can run into the arms of our *Heavenly* Father and experience a real loving relationship, coming boldly to His throne of grace because of Christ (Hebrews 4:16). Yet we also seek to glorify, honor and obey Him as the preeminent and holy God that He is—One who deserves our highest respect. In this, we begin to understand our *why*.

We exist to *glorify* Him and to *enjoy* Him forever.

The Greatest Commandments and The Great Commission

More important than what any catechism says is what *Jesus Himself* said about our purpose. When asked which commandment was the greatest, He responded, saying it is to:

"Love the Lord your God with all your heart and with all your soul and with all your mind and with all your strength."

Then He said:

"The second is this: Love your neighbor as yourself. There is no commandment greater than these."
—Mark 12:30–31

Also, before ascending into heaven, He gave His disciples the Great Commission, telling them to:

"Go and make disciples of all nations, baptizing them in the name of the Father and of the Son and of the Holy Spirit, and teaching them to obey everything I have commanded you."
—Matthew 28:19–20

So, our "why" is rooted in Jesus' own mission statement for us. This is what He made us *for* and calls us *to*:

- **Loving God**
- **Loving Others**
- **& Making Disciples**

We'll discuss these more in depth in relation to our worship ministry context in the upcoming chapters, but let's consider their general meaning here for now.

First, Jesus said we are to love God:

With All Our Heart & Soul

Loving God with our heart and soul, in the Greek, means loving Him with the core of our being—our thoughts, passions, drive, desires, appetites, affections, purposes, and endeavors. It's not about external religious performance or mere lip service, it's about a true and pure inward conviction that leads to action.

God rebuked His people through the prophet Isaiah, saying:

True worship starts in the heart. It is affection and conviction anchored in truth, not emotion detached from Scripture. Our hearts and our will must be set on Him, not just in a moment of singing, but in a lifestyle of devotion.

With All Our Mind

Loving God with our mind means engaging our intellect and reasoning in worship. Faith is not blind. It is intelligent and grounded in truth, and we are called to be diligent like the Bereans in our study and confirmation of what Scripture teaches so we can have a firm foundation for our faith and a clarity of purpose in our worship.

As Paul wrote in **Romans 12:2**:

**Right thinking leads to right living.
Informed worship is the only acceptable worship,
and it all starts by loving God with our minds.**

We don't check our brains at the door when we come to church. The God who created our minds calls us to use them. We love Him by studying to show ourselves approved (1 Timothy 2:15), by meditating on His Word (Psalm 1:2) and by prayerfully asking questions, and thinking deeply about His truth.

To love God with our minds means to filter every idea, philosophy, and opinion through His Word, having a biblical worldview which sees reality as *He* sees it.

With All Our Strength

We also love God with our strength—with our bodies, our energy, and our actions. James tells us we are to be *doers* of the Word, not hearers only, so we serve the Lord. We don't waste our lives. We make them count. Worship manifests itself through loving obedience and works of service unto the Lord and unto others for His glory.

Worship without obedience is empty, but when our songs are matched by surrendered lives, our strength becomes a living testimony of God's power at work in us.

Loving Our Neighbor and Making Disciples

Jesus didn't stop with loving God, He also called us to love *people*. We show our love for God by loving those made in His image. When we see a need, we act. When someone is hurting, we care. When someone is lost, we reach out. Love moves us to give, serve, and share the hope of Jesus.

As worshipers, we're not just musicians, we're also missionaries. Our worship fuels our witness.

One of the greatest joys of the Christian life is found in discipling others, and especially helping others come to know and trust in Christ. It's the one thing we won't be able to do in heaven. We live on mission and share the gospel through our music and through our daily lives as worshipers so that heaven would be full and hell as empty as possible.

The Eternal Perspective

Life is but a breath. This world is temporary, but heaven is eternal.

"What is your life? You are a mist that appears for a little while and then vanishes."
—James 4:14

"The world and its desires pass away,
but whoever does the will of God lives forever."
—1 John 2:17

"So we fix our eyes not on what is seen, but on what is unseen."
—2 Corinthians 4:18

We don't live for earthly applause, fleeting fame, or temporary crowns. We live for the eternal prize—the joy of seeing Jesus face-to-face and hearing Him say, *"Well done, good and faithful servant."*

That's why we worship.

That's why we serve.

That's why we exist, to glorify and enjoy God forever.

Reflection & Discussion Questions

1. What motivates your worship, obligation or delight?
2. Which area of the Greatest Commandment do you find hardest: loving God with your heart, mind, or strength?
3. How can your worship team model loving God and loving people both on and off the platform?
4. What does Paul mean when he says to "be transformed by the renewing of your mind" and how do you do that?
5. How does understanding your "why" change how you approach ministry and worship?

4

WHAT IS WORSHIP?

More Than a Song

For many believers today, the word *worship* has been reduced to something far too small. When people hear the word, they often think of the musical portion of a church service; the singing, the band, the atmosphere, the emotions. While music is a beautiful and biblical expression of worship, it is only one small part of a much bigger picture.

If worship is only something we "do" for 20–30 minutes on a Sunday, then we've missed the heart of what God intended. Worship is not limited to a style, a song, a service, or a moment. It is much more than singing. It is a life lived in *response* to God.

Unfortunately, many incorrectly define worship, and in so doing, they offer to God worthless, false and even offensive offerings. Taking time to define our terms and have a biblical understanding of worship will help us to avoid offering God something He never asked for, and missing the joy of giving Him what He desires most.

Jesus brought clarity to what true worship should look like when He spoke to the Samaritan woman at the well, saying:

*"A time is coming and has now come when the true worshipers will worship the Father **in spirit** and **in truth**, for they are the kind of worshipers the Father seeks."*
—John 4:23–24

God is not looking for performers, spectators, or consumers. He is seeking true worshipers—men and women whose hearts and lives are fully His.

Worship Begins with Revelation

Before we define worship, we must recognize its starting point:

**Worship does not begin with us.
Worship begins with God.**

At its core, worship is a *response*. We are not the initiators of worship. God reveals, and we respond. He speaks, and we answer. He moves, and we offer ourselves.

From Genesis to Revelation, worship always follows this pattern:

Revelation → Response

When God reveals who He is—His character, His power, His nature, His love, and His holiness, worship becomes the natural, joyful, and reasonable response of the human heart.

When Isaiah saw the Lord seated on His throne, high and lifted up, he didn't need to be prompted to worship. The revelation of God's glory overwhelmed him, humbled him, cleansed him, and moved him to surrender (Isaiah 6:1–8). Worship flowed from revelation.

This is why knowing God is at the core of worship. The more clearly we see Him, the more passionately we will worship Him.

Worship Is Our Response

Because worship is a response to God's revelation, we can define it this way:

Worship is our loving, humble, obedient, whole-life response to the revelation of who God is and what He has done for us in Christ.

This definition helps us understand that worship is not passive, emotionally governed, or occasional. It is active, deliberate, and continual. It involves our beliefs, our affections, and our actions. Worship is not something we *attend*, it's something we *live*.

Worship is not fundamentally about what *we* prefer, *we* feel, or *we* enjoy. It's about who God is and what He deserves.

True Worship Is Rooted in the Word

We cannot worship God rightly if we do not know Him accurately, and the only trustworthy revelation of who He is, is found in His Word. Scripture must shape our understanding, expression, and practice of worship.

If we build worship on experience, preference, emotion, or culture, we will drift. If we build worship on Scripture, we will remain anchored in truth.

Jesus prayed:

> *"Sanctify them by the truth; Your Word is truth."*
> —John 17:17

This means worship must be *Word-saturated*, flowing from what God has revealed about Himself. We cannot worship a God we do not know, and we cannot know God apart from His Word. Worship is not shaped by trends or feelings, but by *truth*.

When the Word of God fills our minds, it fuels our hearts and directs our lives into worship.

The Origin of the Word "Worship"

The English word *worship* comes from the Old English term **"worth-ship"**, which means *to declare the worth or value of someone or something*.

This is a good place to start as worship involves recognizing and declaring God's worth, but the Bible gives us a much fuller and richer picture. Worship is not only about what we *say* about God's worth, it's about how we *respond* to His worth through honor, adoration, surrender, obedience, and love.

To build a biblical understanding of worship, we must look at the words that Scripture uses to describe it.

Three Key Biblical Words for Worship

In the Bible, there are three primary words translated into our English word "worship".

1. Shachah (Hebrew)

Meaning: to bow down, to kneel, to lay prostrate before another in reverence

This is the most common Hebrew word for worship in the Old Testament. It conveys a physical posture of humility expressed with the body. To *shachah* is to acknowledge someone's authority, greatness, and superiority by lowering oneself before them.

This posture reflects an attitude of the heart:
God is exalted, and I am humbled before Him.

We see *shachah* throughout Scripture:

- When Abraham "bowed himself to the earth" to show honor and to "worship" the Lord (Genesis 18:2, 22:5)
- When Moses "bowed his head toward the earth and worshiped" (Exodus 34:8)
- When Job "fell to the ground in worship, saying... The Lord gave and the Lord has taken away; blessed be the name of the Lord" (Job 1:20–21)

Worship begins with **humility**—recognizing who God is and responding with surrender and reverence.

Worship is not casual. It calls us to bow low in heart and life, acknowledging God as King.

---

2. Proskuneo (Greek)

Meaning: to bow down and kiss toward; to fall at the feet of one in adoration

Proskuneo is the primary New Testament word for worship and is deeply relational and personal. It pictures a servant kissing the hand of their master or one bowing before a king.

It expresses **adoration, devotion, intimacy, and honor**.

Some examples are:

- When the wise men who traveled an incredible distance "fell down and worshiped [Jesus]." (Matthew 2:11)
- When Jesus healed the man who was born blind, he responded saying, "Lord I believe" and he "worshiped Him." (John 9:38)
- In heaven, the elders fall before the Lamb and worship (Revelation 5:14)

Where *shachah* emphasizes reverence, *proskuneo* emphasizes **relationship** in a loving, heartfelt surrender to the One we adore.

Worship is not cold duty. It is warm devotion. It is the heart drawing near to God in love and honor.

---

3. Latreia (Greek)

Meaning: service or ministry unto God; sacred, priestly service

This word expands worship beyond posture and emotion to **action and obedience**. It is worship expressed through a life of service to God.

Paul uses this word in a decisive verse for understanding worship:

> *"...offer your bodies as a living sacrifice,*
> *holy and pleasing to God—this is your spiritual*
> *and reasonable* latreia *(worship/service)."*
> —*Romans 12:1*

Here, worship is not a moment, but a **lifestyle of loving obedience**. It is serving God with our time, talents, resources, energy, and decisions.

**Worship is not only what we feel or sing,
but what we live and do.
True worship shows up in daily service and obedience.**

Putting It Together

These three words show us a full and biblical picture of worship:

- **Shachah** — to bow in *reverence*
- **Proskuneo** — to draw near in *adoration*
- **Latreia** — to serve in loving *obedience*

Together they show that worship is:

- **Reverent** (God is holy and exalted)
- **Relational** (God is near and to be loved)
- **Responsive** (God is served with our lives)

Worship touches the **mind** (truth), the **heart** (love), and the **life** (obedience).

Worship is a response of humble loving submission and service to the One who first loved us

---

Reflection & Discussion Questions

1. In your own words, how would you define worship based on Chapter 4? How is that different from how you might have defined it five years ago?
2. Reflect on the three key biblical words for worship (*shachah, proskuneo, latreia*). Which one most challenges or corrects your view of worship? Why?
3. Are there any songs, habits, or attitudes in your worship life that are more about *preference* than God's *worth*? How can you lovingly align them more fully with Scripture?
4. For worship leaders/teams: When you plan or lead, do you think more about what is *engaging* or what is *God-exalting and truth-filled*? What would it look like to keep those in the right order?

Take time as a team (or personally) to pray this:

"Lord, teach us to worship You in spirit and in truth. Show us any area that needs to change, and help us respond to You with humility and loving obedience."

5

HOW DO WE WORSHIP?

Now that we've seen what worship truly is—a whole-life response to who God is and what He has done, the question becomes: **How do we live it out?** Worship is not only something we express with our lips, but something we embody with our lives. Scripture doesn't leave us guessing. It gives us a clear picture of what the life of a worshiper looks like.

Worship as a Lifestyle

This clear passage in the Bible describing worship isn't about singing, it's about living. We've made reference to it a few times already in previous chapters and if you haven't committed it to memory yet, I encourage you to do so:

"Therefore, I urge you, brothers and sisters, in view of God's mercy, to offer your bodies as a living sacrifice, holy and pleasing to God—this is your spiritual and reasonable act of worship. Do not conform to the pattern of this world, but be transformed by the renewing of your mind. Then you will be able to test and approve what God's will is—his good, pleasing and perfect will.

—Romans 12:1–2

In this passage, Paul tells us that worship is not merely an activity, it is a **life surrendered to God**. Notice the phrasing: *in view of God's mercy*. Worship begins when we see what God has done for us in Christ and respond by giving Him our whole selves—our thoughts, desires, time, priorities, relationships, and daily choices.

Worship is not confined to the sanctuary. It is lived out in the ordinary and every day.

Worship is:

- Choosing obedience when compromise would be easier
- Loving people who are difficult to love
- Serving when no one notices or applauds
- Keeping your heart tender, repentant, and thankful
- Saying, "Lord, my life belongs to You"—again and again

A worship service on Sunday means very little if it doesn't shape how we live Monday through Saturday.

Worshiping in Spirit and in Truth

When Jesus speaks about worship in John 4, He does more than correct a theological detail. He completely reframes what true worship is.

In His conversation with the Samaritan woman at the well (John 4:1–26), Jesus crosses ethnic, moral, and religious barriers, exposes empty religion and sin, reveals Himself as the long-awaited Messiah, and defines what kind of worshipers the Father is actually seeking. It's a powerful passage and one of my favorite chapters in the Bible.

For Jesus, this moment with the Samaritan woman is not about winning *an argument*. It's about winning *a heart* and showing us what real worship looks like.

The Setting: Broken Worship and a Seeking Savior

The woman at the well comes from Samaria—a region with a complicated and polluted spiritual identity.

The Samaritans had:

- A history of mixed worship (Judaism blended with pagan practices)
- Their own temple on Mount Gerizim
- Only accepted the first five books of Moses while rejecting the Prophets and the Writings

Their religion had fragments of truth, but it was *distorted, incomplete,* and *compromised.*

By contrast, the Jews in Jerusalem had:

- The full Scriptures
- The temple God had appointed
- The promises given through Abraham, Moses, David, and the prophets

So when the woman raises the worship debate, "Our fathers worshiped on this mountain, but you Jews say that the place where we must worship is in Jerusalem" (John 4:20), she's not just talking geography. She's clinging to her system, her tradition, her identity.

Jesus answers with both *clarity* and *compassion.*

*"Believe me, a time is coming when you will worship the Father neither on this mountain nor in Jerusalem. You Samaritans worship what you do not know; we worship what we do know, for salvation is from the Jews. A time is coming and has now come when the true worshipers will worship the Father in spirit and in truth, **for they are the kind of worshipers the Father seeks**. God is spirit, and His worshipers must worship in spirit and in truth."*
—John 4:21–24

In one simple statement, Jesus:

- Affirms that the Jews had the correct revelation ("salvation is from the Jews" v.22)
- Exposes false confidence in sacred places and empty systems
- Announces that worship is not tied to one mountain or city
- Reveals the non-negotiable standard for all true worship going forward

Not Where, but How and Whom

Jesus makes it clear:

It's not ultimately about *where* you worship. It's about *whom* you worship, and *how* you worship Him. The Samaritans had zeal, but not full truth. The Jews had truth, but many lacked heart.

God has always been seeking worshipers whose worship is:

- Not confined to a place
- Not reduced to rituals
- Not based on heritage, feelings, or style
- Rooted in *Spirit and Truth*

Let's unpack that.

Worship in Spirit

"God is spirit," Jesus says (John 4:24). That means:

- He is not confined to a building, mountain, city, or atmosphere.
- He is not accessed by superstition, gimmicks, or empty rituals.
- He is present and to be worshiped wherever His people are.

To worship in **spirit** means:

1. **From the inside out**
   Worship flows from the human spirit, the core of who we are—not just from lips, rituals, or motions.
2. **Genuine, not fake**
   God is not impressed by human performance. He desires sincerity, honesty, humility, repentance, gratitude, and love.
3. **Not limited to songs or settings**
   Worship in spirit may or may not include music.
   It can happen:

- In a car
- In a quiet room with your Bible open
- Washing dishes
- Serving someone in need
- Standing with your church singing loudly

The key is the posture of the heart before God.

It's about your human spirit

connecting with the Spirit of God

in real communion and fellowship.

When we *abide in Christ* by remaining close to Him in prayer, study, faith, obedience, and dependence, He gives rest to our souls and produces lasting spiritual fruit in and through us (John 15:1–5; Matthew 11:28–29, Galatians 5:22).

Worship in spirit is:

- **Relational** (knowing Him)
- **Internal & Supernatural** (spiritual communion)
- **Ongoing** (a way of life, not an event)

Worship in Truth

If "spirit" guards us from mere externals and dead formality, "truth" guards us from vague spirituality. Jesus says the Father is seeking those who worship "in spirit *and* in truth."

To worship in **truth** means:

1. **Rooted in God's Word**
Our worship must align with what God has revealed about Himself in Scripture, not what culture imagines, not what we wish were true, and not what false religion or tradition distorts.

The Samaritans had partial truth mixed with pagan practices, which led to polluted and false worship. Many today have passion but little doctrine, and end up bringing tainted and sometimes even offensive offerings to God as attempted acts of worship. God doesn't want man's idolatrous passion or foolish fleshly efforts. He wants zeal accompanied with knowledge—a burning heart and a biblical mind.

2. **Centered on Christ**
Jesus is "the way, and the truth, and the life" (John 14:6).
All true worship is *Christ-centered* and focused on:

- His person (fully God, fully man)
- His work (cross, resurrection, reign)
- His kingdom
- His Word

If our worship is "spiritual" but not anchored in the Jesus of Scripture, it is not true worship.

3. **Doctrinally Sound**
The lyrics we sing, the prayers we pray, and the teaching we share must reflect sound doctrine.

- We don't sing lies just because the melody is powerful.
- We don't preach ourselves; we preach Christ.
- We measure everything by the Bible.

4. **Aligned with Obedience**
Worshiping in truth is not just knowing the "right facts". It is truth embraced and obeyed. Jesus said in John 14:15, "If you love me, keep my commandments." True theology should lead us to true relationship, gratitude, love, trust and *devotion*. Feelings are much better as followers than leaders. Worshiping in truth means doing what's right according to God's Word, whether it feels good in the moment or not.

Emotions are a gift,

but they must be governed by truth.

When worship is grounded in Scripture:

- Our feelings have a firm foundation
- Our songs proclaim what is real
- Our people are discipled, not just entertained
- Our ministries point clearly to the gospel

Worship in truth protects us from:

- Man-centered songs
- Vague "God talk"
- Emotionalism without substance
- Sincerity that is sincerely wrong

Spirit and Truth Together

Jesus doesn't say "spirit *or* truth." He says "spirit *and* truth." Both are essential.

Truth without **Spirit** becomes cold, rigid, lifeless faux-religion

Spirit without **Truth** can become shallow, unstable, and easily deceived

Spirit and Truth together produce worship that is:

- Alive
- Anchored
- Christ-centered
- Humble
- Fruitful

For worship leaders and teams, this means:

- We must care about *doctrine* and *devotion*
- We must cultivate *theology* and *tenderness*
- We must aim for *clarity* and *fervency*
- We must choose songs, Scriptures, and words that exalt Christ accurately and affectionately

As we personally worship in spirit and in truth, something important happens:

Our inner life with God begins to overflow into *how we live, how we serve, and how we lead.*

This leads us to our next focus, which is:

Worship through Service

When worship is real, it won't remain only internal. It moves us.

Real worship:

- Humbles us before God
- Aligns our hearts with His
- Compels us to love, serve, and obey Him

This is where the biblical idea of **ministry** comes in.

What Does It Mean to Minister?

In everyday English, *to minister* means:

- To attend to the needs of someone
- To care for
- To help
- To provide what is necessary

Like a servant to a king or a doctor to a patient.

In the New Testament we see two Greek words for *Minister*:

- **Leitourgia** —sacred service; an act that serves God and blesses others (where we get "liturgy" and the idea of a "service").
- **Diakonos** —a servant; literally someone so eager to serve they're "kicking up dust" as they go.

Ministry is not about *status,* it is about *service.* Worship and ministry are not separate categories. **Ministry is one of the primary ways we express our worship.**

So the question is no longer just:

"How do I feel when I worship?"

But:

"How do I serve because I worship?"

In the next section of this chapter, we'll explore five key ways worship expresses itself as service:

1. Serving God

2. Serving the Church

3. Serving the Lost

4. Serving the Team

5. Serving the Moment

If our worship in spirit and truth is genuine, it will show up in how we give, love, listen, play, sing, lead, encourage, submit, and serve.

This is how we worship.

If worship in spirit and in truth is real, it will always move us beyond ourselves. Ministry is not about title or spotlight. It is about *serving God and others as an act of worship*.

Jesus said:

> *"The greatest among you will be your **servant**."*
> —Matthew 23:11

> *"The Son of Man did not come to be served, but **to serve**,*
> *and **to give** His life as a ransom for many."*
> —Matthew 20:28

If we claim to follow Jesus, then a *servant's heart* is not optional. We were created to worship, and a massive part of our worship is how we serve.

For pastors, leaders, musicians, techs, creatives, and volunteers, this becomes very practical. Our calling is not just to *do church or songs and production well*, but to love well, serve well, and represent Jesus well.

Let's look at **five key ways** worship expresses itself as service.

1. Serving God

Before we serve anyone else, we serve **God**.

Our first and highest ministry is always *"to the Lord"*. We should love Him, obey Him, honor Him, and seek His pleasure above all.

*"Therefore, I urge you, brothers and sisters, in view of God's mercy, to offer your bodies as a living sacrifice, holy and **pleasing to God**—this is your spiritual and reasonable act of worship."*
—Romans 12:1

Serving God means:

- Prioritizing His *presence* over performance
- Obeying His *Word* even when it costs us
- Checking our *motives*—"Am I doing this to be seen, or to please Him?"
- Being faithful when no one is watching
- Saying, "Lord, this is for *You first*"

For worship teams, serving God looks like:

- Guarding your private walk with Jesus
- Refusing to lead others where you are not willing to go personally
- Letting your setlists, arrangements, visuals, decisions and demeanor be driven by *what most honors the Lord and tells the truth about Him*

When we get this wrong, everything else, even good ministry, can quietly bend around *self*.

When we get this right, *everything else flows out of it.*

2. Serving the Church

Flowing out of our love for God, we joyfully serve His people—
The Church.

*"From Him the whole body, joined and held together by
every supporting ligament, grows and builds itself up
in love, **as each part does its work**."*
—Ephesians 4:16

God gives spiritual gifts *not* so we can showcase ourselves, but
so we can *strengthen the body of Christ*.

Serving the Church as an act of worship means:

- Using our gifts to *build up*, not *show off*
- Making room for others
- Creating spaces where people can see Jesus clearly, hear
  the Word clearly, and respond freely
- Being willing to do unseen tasks with the same joy as
  visible ones

*"Each of you should use whatever gift you have received **to serve**
others, faithfully administering and stewarding God's grace in its
various forms... **so that in all things God may be praised**."*
—1Peter 4:10-11

When we use our gifts to serve the church:

- The body grows in unity and maturity
- Pastors are strengthened and blessed
- People are shepherded, served and strengthened
- God is glorified

That's worship.

3. Serving the Lost

Something happens when unbelievers look on and see us giving thanks to God for His goodness, when they hear songs declaring truth about His power, His holiness and His love that went all the way to the cross for us (while we were still sinners).

When **The Lost** are in our midst and see flawed yet honest and humble people truly worshiping and engaging in relationship and conversation with God—*that atmosphere can really change people.*

Remember David and Saul?

David's heart for God, combined with his soothing musical abilities, changed the atmosphere when the demons plagued Saul. It's crazy, but God really seems to inhabit our praises in a unique and special way, and it can change people.

So as we worship, serve, and live our lives, let's glorify God with the realization that we are on mission whether we're on stage or off of stage, and let's look for opportunities through music, and in our daily lives, to share God's love and the gospel with those who need hope in Christ.

"You are the light of the world... let your light shine before men, that they may see your good deeds and glorify your Father in heaven."

—Matthew 5:14–16

"We are therefore Christ's ambassadors, as though God were making his appeal through us. We implore you on Christ's behalf: Be reconciled to God."

—2 Corinthians 5:20

Serving the lost as an act of worship means:

- Remembering that *real people* are walking in every Sunday carrying sin, pain, confusion, spiritual blindness, hardships, and deep questions
- Recognizing that our words, songs, prayers, excellence, and kindness can help remove obstacles so they can see and hear the Lord clearly
- Connecting with a new or lonely person before or after church
- Finding opportunities outside of church to share the gospel through music and to reach out with your team

"For I am not ashamed of the gospel, for it is the power of God

for salvation to everyone who believes..."

—Romans 1:16

Practically, for worship and tech teams:

- We choose lyrics that are biblically rich and bring gospel-clarity, not just vague spirituality
- We speak and pray in ways that welcome the outsider without watering down the truth
- We care about clarity of sound, slides, lights, flow—not for production's sake, but so people can *focus on Christ* without unnecessary distraction
- We remember that for some, this might be the first time they've truly heard the gospel

We are not performing for people; we are serving before God, for their good.

"Faith comes from hearing the message, and the message is

heard through the word of Christ."

—Romans 10:17

Helping people hear that message is worship.

4. Serving the Team

If we want to lead people in unified worship, our team must embody love, humility, and unity behind the scenes.

"By this everyone will know that you are My disciples, if you love one another."
—John 13:35

"Be completely humble and gentle... Making every effort to keep the unity of the Spirit through the bond of peace."
—Ephesians 4:2–3

Serving **The Team** means:

- Seeing your fellow volunteers as *brothers and sisters*, not competition
- Honoring pastors, leaders, and fellow servants with respect
- Covering one another in prayer
- Choosing encouragement over criticism and solutions over complaints
- Refusing gossip, cliques, or drama
- Being a thermostat—raising the joy, peace, respect and overall attitude and energy in the room and loving well

Some practical ways this can look:

- Celebrate others accomplishments when they do well
- Ask, "Is there anything you need from me this week?"
- Set others up for success with clean charts, audio files, run sheets, cues, transitions, good scheduling and communication
- Be proactive and ask for clarity regarding expectations
- Prepare at home so you don't waste others' time at rehearsal
- Step in to help with setup, teardown, running cables, cleaning backstage or storage areas
- Thank the tech team, bring coffee—be creative!
- Be on-time because you value others' time

When the team is full of humble servants:

- The culture becomes joyful, safe, and strong
- People are drawn to serve, not burned out by it
- The unity on stage reflects the gospel we sing about

That unity *is itself* an act of worship.

5. Serving the Moment

Finally, worshipers who serve well learn to *serve* **The Moment**.

Serving the moment means we are:

- Fully present
- Spiritually-sensitive
- Focused on what God is doing right now in this gathering

It's not about showing off. It's about *stewarding each moment* so that people can clearly see Jesus. Just as John the Baptist said:

"He must become greater; I must become less."

—John 3:30

Serving the moment in gathered worship includes:

- Keeping the focus on Christ, not ourselves
- Playing and leading with passion, but not distraction
- Serving the song so it honors the Lord and best serves people
- Choosing dynamics, transitions, and arrangements that support the song and the overall message and work God is doing each weekend
- Using technical tools (sound, slides, lighting, cameras) to highlight the right thing at the right time
- Putting lyrics on the screen *on time*
- Turning microphones up a little more when someone is praying or speaking as needed
- Not fiddling with your gear unnecessarily during prayer, announcements, or when someone is speaking
- Directing our own attention to the right place at the right time to help lead others and help them stay focused

We ask:

- "What should people be focusing on in *this* moment?"
- "Is what I'm doing helping or distracting?"
- "Am I overplaying?"
- "Can I simplify to help Jesus be the focal point?"

When we serve the moment well:

- People walk away with their eyes on *Jesus*, not on us
- Pastors feel supported and free
- The gathered church experiences an undistracted and edifying environment conducive to corporate prayer and worship in which they can genuinely meet with God

That is worshipful service.

This Is Why We Serve

All of this—Serving God, The Church, The Lost, The Team, and The Moment—is not busywork. It's worship.

This Warren Wiersbe quote about ministry has always stuck with me:

"Ministry takes place when divine resources meet human needs through loving channels to the glory of God."
—*Warren Wiersbe*

I encourage you to break down and consider the meaning of each short phrase within that quote and challenge yourself regularly to live it out. A life dependent on the Holy Spirit to lovingly and willingly do the work of true ministry, produces real edifying spiritual fruit for the glory of God.

Let's look at it again broken down into sections:

Ministry takes place when:

Divine resources (God's grace, goodness, and gifts)

Meet human needs (edification, spiritual impact)

Through loving channels (we are His vessels, the hands and feet of Jesus)

To the glory of God (*God* is glorified for the ministry that takes place)

This idea pairs perfectly with 1 Peter 4:10-11:

"Each of you should use whatever gift you have received to serve others, faithfully stewarding and administering God's grace in its various forms... so that in all things God may be praised."
—1 Peter 4:10-11

What an incredible thing that God, in His kindness, chooses to pour out His love, truth, and grace through ordinary people like you and me, when we humbly say:

"Here I am, Lord. Use me."

As we worship in spirit and in truth, that worship overflows into humble, joyful service, and we begin to reflect the heart of Jesus Himself; the Servant King. May we look more and more like Him. Stewarding and administering God's grace through the gifts He has given us that we might spiritually impact the lives of others and glorify God—*THIS* is true ministry and *THIS* is how we worship.

Reflection & Discussion Questions

1. When you think about your current role (on stage or behind the scenes), do you see it more as *worship* or just *work*? What needs to shift in your perspective?
2. Which of the five areas—Serving God, The Church, The Lost, The Team, or The Moment—do you feel strongest in right now? Which area needs intentional growth?
3. In what ways can you better serve your *team* this month practically, spiritually, or relationally?
4. Think about a recent service. Was there a moment where distraction, sloppiness, or self-focus got in the way? What small changes could help your team serve the moment better next time?
5. Are there any tasks you currently see as "beneath you" or "not your job"? How does Jesus' example of servanthood challenge that attitude?
6. What part of the Warren Wiersbe quote or 1 Peter 4:10-11 stood out to you the most and why?

Take time together (or personally) to pray:
"Lord, teach us to worship You in spirit and in truth, and to express that worship through humble, joyful service in every area You've entrusted to us."

6

THE FIVE C's

Great songs, strong arrangements, tight transitions, and creative environments are good gifts, but they are not everything. A healthy worship ministry strives for these things, but is built on so much more.

In the last chapter we saw that true worship is more than emotion, sound, or setting. We are called to worship in spirit and in truth, and then to express it through a life of service.

In this chapter we'll continue to discuss how the outer expression is formed by the inner spiritual reality and relationship that only God sees; and that *who we are* as worshipers and leaders matters just as much as *what we do*.

That's where the **5 C's** come in:

Character. Competency. Calling. Chemistry. Content.

These aren't meant to be cliché buzzwords. They are practical, biblical categories that help us evaluate our lives and ministries in a way that honors the Lord and serves His church well.

Think of the 5 C's like pillars that support a faithful worship culture. If one collapses, the whole structure is affected.

Let's walk through them.

1. Character

Before God cares about how well you sing, play, mix, design, or lead, He cares about *who you are*.

"Above all else, guard your heart, for everything you do flows from it."
—Proverbs 4:23

In worship ministry, especially for creatives, it's easy to drift into:

- Wanting the platform more than the presence of God
- Craving attention instead of embracing servanthood
- Finding identity in applause, followers, or opportunities instead of Christ

We have to ask honest questions:

- *What is my ambition?*
- *Am I here to serve or to be seen?*
- *Is my identity rooted in Christ or in my gifting?*

A simple warning for every worshiper:

Don't let your talent take you somewhere your character won't sustain you.

Excellence matters, but **character takes precedence**.

People may be impressed by our sound or creativity, but they are only truly impacted long-term by how we live our lives:

- Our humility or pride
- Our purity or compromise
- Our faithfulness or inconsistency
- Our love for people or use of people

Our lives either confirm the message we sing or contradict it.

Some key verses to consider:

- Romans 12:1–2 — Offer your body as a living sacrifice. Be transformed, not conformed to the world
- 1 Timothy 4:12 — Set an example in speech, life, love, faith and purity
- 2 Timothy 2:22 — Flee lusts; pursue righteousness, faith, love and peace
- Galatians 5:22–23 — Produce the fruit of the Spirit
- Colossians 3:17 — Whatever you do, do it in Jesus' name

This includes how we:

- Speak (not using profane, cruel, crude talk)
- Treat people (no objectifying, shaming, belittling)
- Walk in sexuality (honoring God's design)
- Use substances (sober and sober-mindedness)
- Engage online (no public slander, mockery, or division)
- Handle conflict (biblically, humbly)
- Respond when we fail (repentance, not excuses)

Not perfection, but humility, growth, and integrity.

A simple grid:

- Am I abiding in Christ?
- Is the fruit of the Spirit visible in how I live, create, and lead?
- Would I want a younger believer to imitate my lifestyle?

The world doesn't need more epic prodigy superstars and celebrities. It needs men and women of holy, humble, Spirit-formed character who love God, love others and make disciples. That's what changes the world.

---

2. Competency

Character is first, but *competency matters too.*

In many areas of church life, almost anyone who is willing can jump in, learn and begin to serve, but what we do in the area of worship music and production ministry needs some level of gifting and competency for a successful outcome and experience. We must have a bar in order to steward people and the ministry well, because what we do is seen, heard, felt and directly shapes how people engage and receive truth.

Scripture calls us to *skillful* service:

> *"Sing to Him a new song; play **skillfully**, and shout for joy."*
>
> *—Psalm 33:3*

Skill is not about showing off. It is about *serving people well* and *honoring God* with what we offer.

God rebuked His people in Malachi for bringing lame, leftover sacrifices (Malachi 1). The issue wasn't ability; it was a careless attitude and a lack of honor. *He is worthy of our best.*

In worship ministry, competency looks like:

- Using your instrument effectively for its purpose
- Practicing at home so rehearsal is mostly about adding the finishing touches, not learning songs from scratch
- Understanding basic musical foundations (time, tone, dynamics, transitions)
- Being reliable, consistent, and prepared

If you feel underdeveloped, don't be ashamed. Be honest, get coaching, watch training videos, serve in appropriate roles while you grow and ask for feedback. Start simple; fewer songs done well is better than many done poorly.

If you are highly gifted, don't just coast through life. Discipline yourself, steward your gift, train, stretch and refine. Use your strength to *lift others*, not outshine them.

Hard work beats talent

when talent doesn't work hard.

For leaders:

- Build teams where character and growing competency matter more than trendiness or personality
- Start with clean, simple, singable excellence. Add complexity only when the foundation is strong

We're not aiming for perfection or high-level production for its own sake. We're aiming for clarity, faithfulness, stewardship, and love in how we serve God and His people with our skills.

Competency is important for the role that we play in serving the Lord and people.

3. Calling

Competency answers, *"Can* I serve here?"
Calling answers, *"Should* I—and why?"

True calling is not ego, not mere opportunity, not a craving for the stage. It is a response to God's mercy and a surrender to His purposes.

> *"In view of God's mercy... offer your bodies as a living sacrifice..."*
> *—Romans 12:1*

> *"For Christ's love compels us... that those who live should no longer live for themselves but for Him who died for them and was raised again."*
> *—2 Corinthians 5:14–15*

Calling for a worship team member means:

- I see this not as a hobby, but as *kingdom work*
- I understand that my role—instrumental, vocal, tech, visual, pastoral—has *eternal impact*
- I believe God has entrusted gifts to me *to serve others* (1 Peter 4:10–11)
- I am willing to be faithful—even when it's hard, hidden, or unglamorous

Ask yourself:

- *Am I compelled by the love of Christ—or by a desire for a microphone?*
- *If no one thanked me, would I still serve?*
- *If God redirected me to serve in a less visible role, would I obey?*

A healthy sense of calling:

- Produces *ownership* (This matters; I'm in)
- Fuels *perseverance* (I don't quit easily)
- Anchors your heart when seasons shift

We're not just "on the schedule."
We're responding to a holy invitation from The Lord:

"Use your gifts for My glory and My people."

4. Chemistry

You can have people of character, competency, and calling, and still have a difficult, unhealthy team if there is no *chemistry*.

Chemistry is:

- How we relate
- How we work together
- How our personalities, strengths, and weaknesses interact

It's both spiritual and practical.

> *"Make every effort to keep the unity of the Spirit through the bond of peace."*
> *—Ephesians 4:3*

In Acts 15, Paul and Barnabas had such a sharp disagreement that they parted ways. The issue wasn't doctrine; it was *chemistry*. They each wanted different things and wanted to work with different people.

The result?

Two teams went out instead of *one*. Sometimes wisely rearranging teams, roles, or pairings actually produces more fruit.

Healthy chemistry looks like:

- A shared *why* — Jesus, His glory, His people
- Shared values — humility, honor, biblical convictions, servant-heartedness
- Mutual respect — valuing each others' time, gifts, and perspectives
- Relational warmth — you don't have to be best friends who hang out every day, but genuine care helps
- Rhythms together — rehearsing, praying, serving regularly so trust and cohesiveness builds

Unhealthy chemistry looks like:

- Hidden resentment
- Competitiveness
- Sarcasm that wounds
- Passive-aggressive comments
- Ego battles over songs, parts, volume, roles

On a worship or tech team, chemistry is heard and felt in tightness or tension, in joy or strain, and in unity or ego.

Leaders:

- Pay attention to group dynamics
- Protect the team from divisive attitudes
- Confront gossip and pride quickly, but graciously
- Pair people wisely
- Build spaces to pray, laugh, and grow together—not just "run the set"

Team members:

- Be easy to work with
- Be teachable
- Choose encouragement over criticism
- Assume the best (we're all on the same team)
- Remember: the way we relate is part of our worship

Chemistry doesn't mean perfection. It means we are committed to working hard in our role and walking in *love, humility, and unity* as we serve together.

5. Content

The final "C" is crucial:

What are we actually saying, singing, and shaping?

Content matters because:

- Worship forms theology
- Lyrics teach
- Prayers disciple
- Visuals communicate values
- Transitions either clarify or confuse

"Let the message of Christ dwell among you richly as you teach and admonish one another with all wisdom through psalms, hymns, and spiritual songs..."
—Colossians 3:16

Good content is:

- **Christ-centered** — Jesus is the focus, not us
- **God-honoring** — reflects His character and His ways
- **Biblically faithful** — consistent with Scripture, not cliches or distortions for emotional manipulation
- **Edifying** — spiritually strengthens and builds up the church
- **Clear** — understandable, not vague or misleading

We should regularly ask:

- Do our songs clearly point to who God is and what Christ has done?
- Can we defend our lyrics with Scripture?
- Are we more concerned with what is *popular*, or what is *faithful*?
- Are we prioritizing songs that help our people know, love and obey Jesus?

As Matt Redman once warned:

"It's no better to sing a lie than it is to tell a lie."

This doesn't mean we can't use contemporary songs with poetic language, but it does mean we *filter* everything:

- Throw out what is unbiblical
- Gently retire what is shallow or confusing
- Champion content that is doctrinally rich, gospel-rooted, and singable

Content is also bigger than just what's in our music.

- How do we *talk* about God?
- What is the content of our prayers?
- How do we frame Scripture readings and moments of encouragement?
- What do our visuals, stage presence, and body language imply?
- Are we pointing people to a real, holy, gracious Savior or just a vague, nice feeling?

Godly **character** + growing **competency** + clear **calling** + healthy **chemistry** + faithful **content** = a healthy and holy worship culture that will last and produce spiritual fruit.

Reflection & Discussion Questions

1. **Character:** Consider in your own heart: Is there any area of your private life that, if exposed, would undercut your ministry credibility? What step of repentance or accountability do you need to take? (Don't feel pressure to share if you are with a large group. It may be more appropriate to talk with a leader or Christian mentor separately). Strive for building a life and culture of honesty and humble repentance, and help one another grow in holiness and maturity.
2. **Competency:** Where do you need to intentionally grow in skill (music, vocals, tone, gear, tech, planning, communication)? What's one practical step you can take this month?
3. **Calling:** Do you see your role as a temporary task or a God-given stewardship? How do *2 Corinthians 5:14–15* and *1 Peter 4:10-11* challenge your motives?
4. **Chemistry:** Is there any relationship on your team that needs healing, clarification, or forgiveness? What can you do to pursue peace and unity?
5. **Content:** Look at your recent setlists, comments, prayers, scripts, or visuals. Are they clearly Christ-centered and biblically sound? What might need to change?
6. As a team, which of the **5 C's** is your greatest strength? Which is your greatest risk if ignored?

Take time to pray together:
"Lord, shape our character, sharpen our competency, confirm our calling, strengthen our chemistry, and purify our content for Your glory and for the good of Your church."

7

THE FIVE P's

As worship leaders, pastors, musicians, and volunteers, one of our greatest weekly responsibilities is shepherding God's people and stewarding the moment when God's people gather.

We're not just picking songs we like. We're helping form hearts, shape theology, encourage faith, and proclaim the gospel to believers and unbelievers through everything we sing, say, and structure.

Two passages give us a clear framework for what should characterize our gathered worship:

"Speak to one another with psalms, hymns, and spiritual songs. Sing and make music from your heart to the Lord, always giving thanks to God the Father for everything in the name of our Lord Jesus Christ."
—Ephesians 5:19–20

"Let the word of Christ dwell in you richly as you teach and admonish one another with all wisdom through psalms, hymns, and spiritual songs, singing to God with gratitude in your hearts. And whatever you do... do it all in the name of the Lord Jesus, giving thanks to God the Father through Him."
—Colossians 3:16–17

Our songs are meant to be:

- Word-filled
- Christ-centered
- Vertical (prayers and communion with the Lord)
- Horizontal (encouraging and instructing one another)
- Saturated with gratitude
- Motivating to mission

To help aim for that kind of balance, I like to think in terms of what I call **"The 5 P's"**.

In every worship set and every weekend gathering, I want to intentionally incorporate as many of these as I can:

1. Power

2. Praise

3. Propitiation

4. Prayer

5. Purpose

These five themes help us honor God, serve the church, and reach the unbeliever—with clarity.

We'll look at each with a biblical anchor and consider practical implications for planning.

1. Power

Definition:
Songs, readings, and moments that declare the **greatness** of God—
His holiness, wisdom, love, faithfulness, and power.

We often begin here in our worship sets, and rightly so.

Corporate worship should regularly lift people's eyes from
themselves, their week, their fears, and their circumstances to
behold the God who created all things, rules over all things, holds all
things together, and is mighty to save.

"Great is the Lord and most worthy of praise; His greatness no one can fathom."

—Psalm 145:3

"Ah, Sovereign LORD, You have made the heavens and the earth by

Your great power and outstretched arm. Nothing is too hard for You."

—Jeremiah 32:17

When we declare His power and greatness:

- Believers are strengthened and reminded to whom they belong
- Unbelievers hear a clear, bold witness of the God we worship
- Fear, pride, and apathy are confronted by the reality of His majesty

In Your Worship Set

Incorporate songs and Scriptures that:

- Exalt God's character (holy, powerful, faithful, and near)
- Declare His works (creation, redemption, faithfulness to His people)
- Stir awe and confidence

These "Power" moments help set a *God-centered tone* from the start.

Praise

Definition:
Songs and expressions that give glory to God with **gratitude, adoration, and thanksgiving** for who He is and what He has done.

If "Power" declares His greatness, "Praise" responds with thankful hearts.

> *"Enter His gates with thanksgiving and His courts with praise;*
> *give thanks to Him and praise His name.*
> *For the LORD is good and His love endures forever."*
> *—Psalm 100:4–5*

> *"Through Jesus, therefore, let us continually offer to God a sacrifice of*
> *praise—the fruit of lips that openly profess His name."*
> *—Hebrews 13:15*

As leaders, we want our gatherings to train the church to **thank God** often and openly:

- For salvation
- For His faithfulness
- For His daily mercies and provision
- For answered prayers
- Even for trials that He uses for good

In Your Worship Set

Include songs that:

- Simply adore God for His goodness
- Express joy and gratitude
- Celebrate His love, kindness, and faithfulness

Don't underestimate the witness of a thankful people. When unbelievers see us sincerely thanking God, it testifies that He is real, active, and worthy of trust.

Propitiation

Definition:
Songs and teachings that clearly proclaim Christ's **atoning work on the cross**—that He bore our sin, satisfied the righteous wrath of God, and reconciled us to Himself.

This is a big word, but a vital reality. Biblical worship must be centered on the cross. If our services are filled with emotion and passion, but lack the gospel, we've missed the whole point.

"God presented Christ as a sacrifice of atonement [propitiation] through the shedding of His blood—to be received by faith."
—Romans 3:25

"He Himself is the propitiation for our sins, and not for ours only but also for the whole world."
—1 John 2:2

"God made Him who had no sin to be sin for us, so that in Him we might become the righteousness of God."
—2 Corinthians 5:21

We need songs and moments that regularly:

- Name sin as sin
- Lift up Jesus as the only Savior
- Proclaim the cross, the blood, the resurrection, and grace
- Invite repentance and faith

In Your Worship Set

Intentionally weave in at least one song, scripture, prayer or brief exhortation that explicitly proclaims the gospel and points to the cross.

This serves:

- Believers, by grounding their praise in the finished work of Christ
- Unbelievers, by clearly presenting the way of salvation
- The whole church, by keeping Jesus' sacrifice central

A set without the cross may feel inspiring, but it will not be *distinctly Christian.*

Prayer

Definition:
Songs and moments that give voice to **personal and corporate prayer**—dependence, confession, surrender, intercession, and desire for God.

Worship is not only declaring who God is, it is also *talking with Him*.

Our gatherings should make space for:

- Calling on the Lord
- Casting our cares on Him
- Confessing sin and weakness
- Asking for personal revival, empowering, and direction
- Expressing hunger for more of Him

"Cast all your cares on Him because He cares for you."
—1 Peter 5:7

"Do not be anxious about anything, but in every situation, by prayer and petition, with thanksgiving, present your requests to God."
—Philippians 4:6

The Psalms are full of sung prayers—honest, raw, and reverent:

- "Search me, O God" (Psalm 139)
- "Create in me a clean heart" (Psalm 51)
- "Lead me to the rock that is higher than I" (Psalm 61)

In Your Worship Set

You can cultivate "Prayer" by using songs that are clearly prayers ("Lord, I need You...", "Have Your way...", "Speak, O Lord..."), and by building in intentional moments of spoken or silent prayer between or during songs, allowing space for the congregation to respond personally to what they've heard.

This reminds the church, and shows the watching world, that our God is not distant; He is a Father who listens, cares, leads, comforts, convicts, and answers our prayers.

Purpose

Definition:
Songs of **response** that call people to **live out** what they've just learned or sung—obedience, mission, surrender, holiness, love, and going into the world for His glory.

If we only declare truth, but never *respond* with our lives, we've stopped short of true and full worship.

"Purpose" songs and moments help the church say:

- "Because of who You are and what You've done, we will follow"
- "Send us"
- "Use us"
- "Our lives belong to You"

"Therefore, I urge you, brothers and sisters, in view of God's mercy, to offer your bodies as a living sacrifice..."
—Romans 12:1

"Do not merely listen to the word, and so deceive yourselves. Do what it says."
—James 1:22

"Go and make disciples of all nations..."
—Matthew 28:19

"Purpose" in a worship set sounds like:

- Consecration
- Surrender
- Mission
- "Here I am, send me"

In Your Worship Set

Think of your final song, prayer or send-off moment as:

- A *response*, not just a closer
- A chance to help people move from *hearing* to *doing*

Examples conceptually:

- "I will follow You…"
- "Take my life and let it be…"
- "Lead me in Your love to those around me…"
- "I desire to worship and obey…"

These moments help seal the word in people's hearts and send them out as worshipers and witnesses.

Worship is not just what happens in the room. It's the life we live when we walk out the doors.

Why the 5 P's Matter

When we think and plan with **Power, Praise, Propitiation, Prayer, and Purpose** in mind, we are:

- Magnifying God clearly
- Feeding the church a full, healthy "theological diet"
- Witnessing to unbelievers
- Giving language for hearts, minds, and lives to respond to God
- Helping our sets reflect the breadth of biblical worship—not just one emotional note

Not every service will feature each "P" with equal weight, and that's okay, but over time, aiming for this balance helps us:

- Stay centered on Christ and the cross
- Avoid self-centered or vague worship
- Keep our gatherings rich in Scripture, gospel, dependence, and mission

Music is powerful. It shapes what people feel, remember, and believe.

So let's steward that power with intention, using our songs and structures to:

- **Exalt the greatness of God (Power)**
- **Thank and adore Him (Praise)**
- **Lift high the cross and the resurrection (Propitiation)**
- **Call on Him—Confess, repent and depend on Him (Prayer)**
- **Send His people out to live obedient, missional lives (Purpose)**

This is how we help our churches worship in spirit and in truth—week after week.

Reflection & Team Discussion Questions

1. Looking at your recent worship sets, which of the 5 P's have been most present? Which have been missing or weak?
2. Do your gatherings clearly communicate the *gospel* (Propitiation), or is it often assumed but unsung/unsaid?
3. How can you build more intentional (Prayer) into your services (sung or spoken), not just as transitions, but as worship?
4. Are your songs more focused on what God does for us or also on who He is and how we should respond (Purpose)?
5. As a team, try planning an upcoming set with the 5 P's in mind. Afterward, discuss: How did it shape the flow, focus, and fruit of the gathering?
6. What small adjustments could you make this month to help your worship ministry better honor God, serve the church, and reach unbelievers through these five lenses?

8

TEAM VALUES

If worship is more than music, and ministry is more than a platform, then *who we are as a team* matters just as much as what we do.

The goal is not to build a group of performers. The goal is to cultivate a family of *servant-hearted worshipers* who reflect Jesus on and off the stage.

As servant-leaders and worship team members, we want to be:

1. HUMBLE

2. COACHABLE

3. COMPELLED

4. CARING

5. COMFORTABLE IN OUR OWN SKIN

6. RESILIENT

7. HONORING

8. SERVANT-HEARTED

These are not just nice ideas. They are *biblical values* that help shape a healthy culture.

Let's walk through each one.

1. HUMBLE

Humility is first on purpose.

God is not impressed with our talent, our tone, or our technology, and pride is detrimental to any ministry. Over and over, Scripture makes it clear:

"God opposes the proud but gives grace to the humble."
—James 4:6

"This is the one I esteem: he who is humble and contrite in spirit, and trembles at My word."
—Isaiah 66:2

Humility is:

- Thinking rightly about ourselves in light of who God is
- Remembering we are loved, but also sinful and in need of grace
- Refusing to be the hero of the story

Questions to ask:

- Am I a *servant* or am I seeking a spotlight?
- Do I *promote others* or mostly promote myself?
- Do I let others praise me, or do I praise myself?

A humble team member:

- Listens
- Shares credit
- Owns mistakes
- Continually points people to Jesus, not themselves

This is the kind of heart God esteems, and the kind of heart people love to follow.

2. COACHABLE

If we're going to grow, we must be coachable and willing to be molded, mentored, and shaped by the Lord and others.

Scripture is blunt:

"To learn, you must love discipline; it is stupid to hate correction."
—Proverbs 12:1

"Wounds from a friend can be trusted, but an enemy multiplies kisses."
—Proverbs 27:6

"As iron sharpens iron, so one person sharpens another.'
—Proverbs 27:17

Being coachable means:

- I can learn from leadership, teammates, and from those I lead
- I can receive feedback without getting defensive or falling apart
- I can adjust how I play, sing, speak, dress, or lead for the sake of the team and the church
- I believe correction is meant to *help* me, not *hurt* me

Proverbs 9 says the wise person *loves* correction, but the mocker resents it.

On a worship team, coachable people ask for honest feedback, listen and look for ways to learn, serve, and grow, and say "thank you" when coached or corrected.

Un-coachable people make excuses, blame others, get defensive and *react* rather than listen and *respond,* and end up staying stuck.

It's not always easy to receive criticism, but let's seek to have *thick skin and soft hearts,* being able to hear hard things, allow God to mold us, and walk in love toward all.

3. COMPELLED

As believers, we aren't called to be a *driven* people in the sense of accomplishing our goals at all costs. We are to be a *compelled* people. We don't labor to gain a name for ourselves or perform from a competitive need to win. Nor do we serve out of guilt, pressure, or hype. We work as unto the Lord (Colossians 3:23) and we serve because we are *compelled by the love of Christ.*

*"For **Christ's love compels us**... that those who live should no longer live for themselves but for Him who died for them and was raised again."*
—2 Corinthians 5:14–15

*"When I preach the gospel, I cannot boast, since **I am compelled** to preach. Woe to me if I do not preach the gospel!"*
—1 Corinthians 9:16

A compelled heart says:

- "After what Jesus has done for me, how could I not respond?"
- "I want people to know Him, be reconciled to Him, and stand in awe of Him"

Being compelled means:

- We are motivated by *love*, not ego
- We want the church to be strengthened and matured
- We care about lost people hearing the gospel
- We see our songs and our service as part of God's *ministry of reconciliation and discipleship*

We're not just filling slots. We're partnering with God to help restore hearts to Him.

4. CARING

Ministry is people work. If we can play skillfully but don't love people well, we've missed the heart of Jesus.

"Truly I tell you, whatever you did for one of the least of these brothers and sisters of mine, you did for me (Jesus)"
—Matthew 25:40

"Carry each other's burdens, and in this way you will fulfill the law of Christ".
—Galatians 6:2

"Love your neighbor as yourself."
—Mark 12:31

"Each of you should look not only to your own interests, but also to the interests of others... have the same mindset as Christ Jesus."
—Philippians 2:4–5

Jesus, God with us, took the form of a servant and came to reach and care for us, and we are to follow in His footsteps.

Being caring means we are:

- Warm, approachable, and kind
- Aware of the people around us
- Willing to listen, pray, and help
- Focused on edifying people instead of impressing them

People may not remember our exact set list, but they will remember:

- Whether they felt seen
- Whether someone followed up
- Whether our team culture had the heart of Jesus

Let's be a team that genuinely cares.

5. COMFORTABLE IN OUR OWN SKIN

In a comparison culture and platform-heavy environment, it's easy to become performers instead of sons and daughters.

But in Christ, we are *already accepted.*

"We are God's workmanship, created in Christ Jesus to do good works, which God prepared in advance for us to do."
—*Ephesians 2:10*

"I praise You because I am fearfully and wonderfully made."
—*Psalm 139:14*

"Am I now trying to win the approval of human beings, or of God? If I were still trying to please people, I would not be a servant of Christ."
—*Galatians 1:10*

Being comfortable in our own skin means:

- We don't have to wear Saul's armor (1 Samuel 17)
- We know our identity is in Christ, not in our role
- We don't have to copy other churches, leaders, or celebrities
- We aren't crushed by comparison or people-pleasing
- We are free to grow into the *best Spirit-led version* of who God made us to be

We can embrace and grow in our gifts and calling, following God's leading without fear, because our worth is secure in Him.

6. RESILIENT

Ministry is beautiful—*and* brutal.

Spiritual warfare is real, criticism happens, schedules are busy, things go wrong, feelings get hurt, technology fails, people leave.

If we're going to last, we need a *holy resilience*.

> *"We are hard pressed on every side, but not crushed…*
> *struck down, but not destroyed."*
> —2 Corinthians 4:8–9

> *"Our struggle is not against flesh and blood…"*
> —Ephesians 6:12

> *"Submit yourselves, then, to God.*
> *Resist the devil, and he will flee from you."*
> —James 4:7

Resilient team members:

- Expect opposition without being shocked by it
- Don't crumble at every bump
- Stay steady when plans change
- Keep a joyful, faith-filled attitude
- Pray, repent, adjust, and keep going

Questions:

- Can I take a hit and not quit?
- Do I lean into God when I'm tired, misunderstood, or discouraged?
- Do I believe that what God has called me to, He will sustain me through?

We want to be people who are not made of glass, but who fight the good fight, grounded in grace.

7. HONORING

An honoring culture is rare and powerful.

"Be devoted to one another in love.
Honor one another above yourselves."
—Romans 12:10

"In humility value others above yourselves."
—Philippians 2:3

To honor is to:

- Treat people as image-bearers of God
- Show respect to leaders, teammates, and those we lead
- Celebrate others' wins
- Not grumble and complain about people
- Not publicly shame others
- Share concerns and feedback respectfully
- Assume the best instead of the worst

Practically, this means:

- We "honor up" (leaders)
- We "honor down" (those we lead or host)
- We "honor all around" (teammates, staff, volunteers, and the congregation)

On a worship team, that looks like:

- Honoring pastoral direction
- Honoring tech teams and support roles
- Honoring younger or less experienced players
- Honoring the congregation by serving them well

An honoring team is approachable, safe, and unified.

8. SERVANT-HEARTED

All the other values point here.

If we are humble, coachable, compelled, caring, secure, resilient, and honoring, we will also be *servant-hearted*, following the example of Jesus.

*"For even the Son of Man did not come to be served, but **to serve**, and to give His life as a ransom for many."*
—Mark 10:45

*"Each of you should use whatever gift you have received **to serve** others, as faithful stewards of God's grace."*
—1 Peter 4:10

A servant-hearted person:

- Asks, "What needs to be done?" not "What do I feel like doing?"
- Is willing to stack chairs, run cables, hold doors, pray quietly, lean in or step back when needed
- Sees every role—on stage, off stage, in any area of church and in every area of life—as worship unto God

We follow a King who washed feet.

No one on the team is above serving.

Leaders go first.

"Attitude reflects leadership, captain."
—Julius Campbell
(Remember The Titans)

Bringing It Together

As servant-leaders and worship team members, we want to be:

HUMBLE — low before God, yet secure in His love
COACHABLE — willing to grow and correctable
COMPELLED — motivated by Christ's love and the gospel
CARING — genuinely loving people we serve and serve with
COMFORTABLE IN OUR OWN SKIN — identity in Christ, not performance
RESILIENT — steady under pressure, trusting God in the battle
HONORING — showing respect and value to all
SERVANT-HEARTED — following Jesus' example in everything

This is the kind of team God can trust with people.
This is the kind of culture that makes much of Jesus.

Reflection & Discussion Questions

1. Which of these eight values most naturally describes you?
    Which one challenges you the most?
2. Where have you seen pride, insecurity, or un-coachability
    damage team culture? What can be learned from that?
3. How can your team grow in caring for each other and for the
    congregation beyond the platform?
4. What does resilience look like for your team in this season?
    How can you better prepare your hearts for distractions,
    technical issues, spiritual opposition and hardship?
5. What is one specific way your team can practice honor and
    servant-heartedness this month (toward pastors, tech teams,
    new volunteers, or the congregation)?

As a team, pray through each value and ask the Lord: "Show us
where we reflect this well, and where You want to grow us."

9

MUSIC IN THE BIBLE

Introduction

As a bit of bonus material, I wanted to add these last two chapters to help us see the power of music and what some honest and healthy creative expressions look like biblically. This is not an exhaustive list of all the songs in the Bible, but simply some key moments of declaration, praise and prayer that have captivated the hearts of saints for generations. Some were spontaneous and some were written slowly and thoughtfully as a response to specific events, which shows there's not just one way to create, communicate or respond to God.

After we explore these, we will close the book by looking at some practical ways to best prepare and serve our teams and congregations in the final chapter. As you consider some of the songs and expressions highlighted here, you can also see how the themes of the Five P's (Power, Praise, Propitiation, Prayer, and Purpose) were utilized by the writers as well. For instance, in Psalm 105:1-5, I see this:

¹ Give praise to the LORD **(praise)**, call on his name **(prayer)**;
    make known among the nations **(purpose)** what he has done **(power)**.
² Sing to him **(purpose)**, sing praise to him **(praise)**;
    tell of **(purpose)** all his wonderful acts **(power)**.
³ Glory in his holy name **(praise)**;
    let the hearts of those who seek the LORD **(prayer)** rejoice **(praise)**.
⁴ Look to the LORD **(prayer)** and his strength **(power)**;
    seek his face always **(prayer)**.
⁵ Remember **(purpose)** the wonders he has done **(power)**,
    his miracles, and the judgments he pronounced **(power)**.

You can consider the Five P's as you read each of the songs and expressions in this chapter or you can pick just one at the end to discuss with your team or small group.

Music in the Old Testament

The Song Of Moses and The Song of Miriam

The "Song of Moses" in Exodus 15 is the first song recorded in the Bible. It was a spontaneous expression of praise and gratitude and a declaration of the character and power of God after He parted the Red Sea to save them from the Egyptians. Then, immediately following Moses' song, Miriam led the women in a musical response with tambourines and dancing to celebrate their freedom. This event set a precedent for how music would be used in Israelite worship—as a way to recount and celebrate God's saving actions.

Moses and the Israelites sang this song to the LORD:

*[1] I will sing to the LORD,
for he is highly exalted;
he has thrown the horse
and its rider into the sea.
[2] The LORD is my strength and my song;
he has become my salvation.
This is my God, and I will praise him,
my father's God, and I will exalt him.*

*[3] The LORD is a warrior;
the LORD is his name.
[4] He threw Pharaoh's chariots
and his army into the sea;
the elite of his officers
were drowned in the Red Sea.
[5] The floods covered them;
they sank to the depths like a stone.*

6 LORD, your right hand is glorious in power.
LORD, your right hand shattered the enemy.
7 You overthrew your adversaries
by your great majesty.
You unleashed your burning wrath;
it consumed them like stubble.
8 The water heaped up at the blast from your nostrils;
the currents stood firm like a dam.
The watery depths congealed in the heart of the sea.

9 The enemy said:
"I will pursue, I will overtake,
I will divide the spoil.
My desire will be gratified at their expense.
I will draw my sword;
my hand will destroy them."

10 But you blew with your breath,
and the sea covered them.
They sank like lead
in the mighty waters.
11 LORD, who is like you among the gods?
Who is like you, glorious in holiness,
revered with praises, performing wonders?
12 You stretched out your right hand,
and the earth swallowed them.

13 With your faithful love,
you will lead the people
you have redeemed;
you will guide them to your holy dwelling
with your strength.
14 When the peoples hear, they will shudder;
anguish will seize the inhabitants of Philistia.
15 Then the chiefs of Edom will be terrified;
trembling will seize the leaders of Moab;

¹⁹ When Pharaoh's horses with his chariots and horsemen went into the sea, the LORD brought the water of the sea back over them. But the Israelites walked through the sea on dry ground.

²⁰ Then the prophetess Miriam, Aaron's sister, took a tambourine in her hand, and all the women came out following her with tambourines and dancing. ²¹ Miriam sang to them:

The Song of Deborah

In Judges 5, Deborah, the prophetess and judge, along with Barak, the military commander, sing a hymn celebrating the Israelites' defeat of the Canaanite army. They praise God for the victory, declaring His divine power and intervention while also praising the leaders and tribes who fought together, and then chiding the tribes that didn't participate:

[1] On that day Deborah and Barak son of Abinoam sang this song:

[2] *"When the princes in Israel take the lead,*
    when the people willingly offer themselves—
    praise the LORD!
[3] *"Hear this, you kings! Listen, you rulers!*
    I, even I, will sing to the LORD;
    I will praise the LORD, the God of Israel, in song.
[4] *"When you, LORD, went out from Seir,*
    when you marched from the land of Edom,
the earth shook, the heavens poured,
    the clouds poured down water.
[5] *The mountains quaked before the LORD, the One of Sinai,*
    before the LORD, the God of Israel.
[6] *"In the days of Shamgar son of Anath,*
    in the days of Jael, the highways were abandoned;
    travelers took to winding paths.
[7] *Villagers in Israel would not fight;*
    they held back until I, Deborah, arose,
    until I arose, a mother in Israel.
[8] *God chose new leaders*
    when war came to the city gates,
but not a shield or spear was seen
    among forty thousand in Israel.
[9] *My heart is with Israel's princes,*
    with the willing volunteers among the people.
    Praise the LORD!
[10] *"You who ride on white donkeys,*
    sitting on your saddle blankets,
    and you who walk along the road,
consider [11] *the voice of the singers at the watering places.*
    They recite the victories of the LORD,
    the victories of his villagers in Israel.
"Then the people of the LORD
    went down to the city gates.
[12] *'Wake up, wake up, Deborah!*

Wake up, wake up, break out in song!
Arise, Barak!
Take captive your captives, son of Abinoam.'
13 *"The remnant of the nobles came down;*
the people of the LORD came down to me against the mighty.
14 *Some came from Ephraim, whose roots were in Amalek;*
Benjamin was with the people who followed you.
From Makir captains came down,
from Zebulun those who bear a commander's staff.
15 *The princes of Issachar were with Deborah;*
yes, Issachar was with Barak,
sent under his command into the valley.
In the districts of Reuben
there was much searching of heart.
16 *Why did you stay among the sheep pens[d]*
to hear the whistling for the flocks?
In the districts of Reuben
there was much searching of heart.
17 *Gilead stayed beyond the Jordan.*
And Dan, why did he linger by the ships?
Asher remained on the coast
and stayed in his coves.
18 *The people of Zebulun risked their very lives;*
so did Naphtali on the terraced fields.
19 *"Kings came, they fought,*
the kings of Canaan fought.
At Taanach, by the waters of Megiddo,
they took no plunder of silver.
20 *From the heavens the stars fought,*
from their courses they fought against Sisera.
21 *The river Kishon swept them away,*
the age-old river, the river Kishon.
March on, my soul; be strong!
22 *Then thundered the horses' hooves—*
galloping, galloping go his mighty steeds.

23 *'Curse Meroz,' said the angel of the LORD.*
   'Curse its people bitterly,
because they did not come to help the LORD,
   to help the LORD against the mighty.'
24 *"Most blessed of women be Jael,*
   the wife of Heber the Kenite,
   most blessed of tent-dwelling women.
25 *He asked for water, and she gave him milk;*
   in a bowl fit for nobles she brought him curdled milk.
26 *Her hand reached for the tent peg,*
   her right hand for the workman's hammer.
She struck Sisera, she crushed his head,
   she shattered and pierced his temple.
27 *At her feet he sank,*
   he fell; there he lay.
At her feet he sank, he fell;
   where he sank, there he fell—dead.
28 *"Through the window peered Sisera's mother;*
   behind the lattice she cried out,
'Why is his chariot so long in coming?
   Why is the clatter of his chariots delayed?'
29 *The wisest of her ladies answer her;*
   indeed, she keeps saying to herself,
30 *'Are they not finding and dividing the spoils:*
   a woman or two for each man,
colorful garments as plunder for Sisera,
   colorful garments embroidered,
highly embroidered garments for my neck—
   all this as plunder?'
31 *"So may all your enemies perish, LORD!*
   But may all who love you be like the sun
   when it rises in its strength."

Then the land had peace forty years.

David and Saul

In 1 Samuel 16:23, music (and possibly the presence of the Lord with David) somehow brought relief to Saul from the evil spirit that was upon him. It's a little mysterious, but worth noting:

23 Whenever the evil spirit from God came upon Saul, David would pick up his lyre and play. Saul would then be relieved and the evil spirit would leave him.

David and the Ark

In 1 Chronicles 16 and 2 Samuel 6, when the Ark was being brought to Jerusalem—this time in the prescribed way, David and the Levites gave praise to God and celebrated unashamedly. Singing and dancing without his royal robes, David worshiped alongside the commoners setting an example of humility and gratitude before God. His wife Michal, who was Saul's daughter, considered his public display undignified for a king. She confronted him, saying he had shamelessly uncovered himself in front of the people, but David replied that he was celebrating before the Lord. As the daughter of a king and the wife of a king, she was embarrassed by David's uninhibited joy. She saw his dancing and the removal of his royal robes as a public disgrace that lowered the dignity of the throne. David explained that his actions were a celebratory expression of worship before God, not a display of royal dignity. He felt it was important to become undignified in his own eyes to honor the Lord, which King Saul famously did not do.

They brought the ark of God and set it inside the tent that David had pitched for it, and they presented burnt offerings and fellowship offerings before God. ²After David had finished sacrificing the burnt offerings and fellowship offerings, he blessed the people in the name of the LORD. ³ Then he gave a loaf of bread, a cake of dates and a cake of raisins to each Israelite man and woman.

⁴ He appointed some of the Levites to minister before the ark of the LORD, to extol, thank, and praise the LORD, the God of Israel: ⁵ Asaph was the chief, and next to him in rank were Zechariah, then Jaaziel, Shemiramoth, Jehiel, Mattithiah, Eliab, Benaiah, Obed-Edom and Jeiel. They were to play the lyres and harps, Asaph was to sound the cymbals, ⁶ and Benaiah and Jahaziel the priests were to blow the trumpets regularly before the ark of the covenant of God.

⁷ That day David first appointed Asaph and his associates to give praise to the LORD in this manner:

⁸ *Give praise to the LORD, proclaim his name;*
make known among the nations what he has done.
⁹ *Sing to him, sing praise to him;*
tell of all his wonderful acts.
¹⁰ *Glory in his holy name;*
let the hearts of those who seek the LORD rejoice.
¹¹ *Look to the LORD and his strength;*
seek his face always.
¹² *Remember the wonders he has done,*
his miracles, and the judgments he pronounced,
¹³ *you his servants, the descendants of Israel,*
his chosen ones, the children of Jacob.
¹⁴ *He is the LORD our God;*
his judgments are in all the earth.
¹⁵ *He remembers his covenant forever,*
the promise he made, for a thousand generations,
¹⁶ *the covenant he made with Abraham,*
the oath he swore to Isaac.
¹⁷ *He confirmed it to Jacob as a decree,*
to Israel as an everlasting covenant:
¹⁸ *"To you I will give the land of Canaan*
as the portion you will inherit."

19 When they were but few in number,
*   few indeed, and strangers in it,*
20 they wandered from nation to nation,
*   from one kingdom to another.*
21 He allowed no one to oppress them;
*   for their sake he rebuked kings:*
22 "Do not touch my anointed ones;
*   do my prophets no harm."*
23 Sing to the LORD, all the earth;
*   proclaim his salvation day after day.*
24 Declare his glory among the nations,
*   his marvelous deeds among all peoples.*
25 For great is the LORD and most worthy of praise;
*   he is to be feared above all gods.*
26 For all the gods of the nations are idols,
*   but the LORD made the heavens.*
27 Splendor and majesty are before him;
*   strength and joy are in his dwelling place.*
28 Ascribe to the LORD, all you families of nations,
*   ascribe to the LORD glory and strength.*
29 Ascribe to the LORD the glory due his name;
*   bring an offering and come before him.*
*   Worship the LORD in the splendor of his holiness.*
30 Tremble before him, all the earth!
*   The world is firmly established; it cannot be moved.*
31 Let the heavens rejoice, let the earth be glad;
*   let them say among the nations, "The LORD reigns!"*
32 Let the sea resound, and all that is in it;
*   let the fields be jubilant, and everything in them!*
33 Let the trees of the forest sing,
*   let them sing for joy before the LORD,*
*   for he comes to judge the earth.*
34 Give thanks to the LORD, for he is good;
*   his love endures forever.*
35 Cry out, "Save us, God our Savior;

gather us and deliver us from the nations,
that we may give thanks to your holy name,
and glory in your praise."
36 *Praise be to the LORD, the God of Israel,*
from everlasting to everlasting.

Then all the people said "Amen" and "Praise the LORD."

37 David left Asaph and his associates before the ark of the covenant of the LORD to minister there regularly, according to each day's requirements. **38** He also left Obed-Edom and his sixty-eight associates to minister with them. Obed-Edom son of Jeduthun, and also Hosah, were gatekeepers.

39 David left Zadok the priest and his fellow priests before the tabernacle of the LORD at the high place in Gibeon **40** to present burnt offerings to the LORD on the altar of burnt offering regularly, morning and evening, in accordance with everything written in the Law of the LORD, which he had given Israel. **41** With them were Heman and Jeduthun and the rest of those chosen and designated by name to give thanks to the LORD, "for his love endures forever." **42** Heman and Jeduthun were responsible for the sounding of the trumpets and cymbals and for the playing of the other instruments for sacred song. The sons of Jeduthun were stationed at the gate.

43 Then all the people left, each for their own home, and David returned home to bless his family.

2 Samuel 6:12-23 gives us a few more details:

David went and had the ark of God brought up from Obed-Edom's house to the city of David with rejoicing. **13** When those carrying the ark of the LORD advanced six steps, he sacrificed an ox and a fattened calf. **14** David was dancing with all his might before the LORD wearing a linen ephod. **15** He and the whole house of Israel were bringing up the ark of the LORD with shouts and the sound of the ram's horn. **16** As the ark of the LORD was entering the city of David, Saul's daughter Michal looked down from the window and saw King David leaping and dancing before the LORD, and she despised him in her heart.

¹⁷ They brought the ark of the LORD and set it in its place inside the tent David had pitched for it. Then David offered burnt offerings and fellowship offerings in the LORD's presence. ¹⁸ When David had finished offering the burnt offering and the fellowship offerings, he blessed the people in the name of the LORD of Hosts. ¹⁹ Then he distributed a loaf of bread, a date cake, and a raisin cake to each one in the entire Israelite community, both men and women. Then all the people went home.

²⁰ When David returned home to bless his household, Saul's daughter Michal came out to meet him. "How the king of Israel honored himself today!" she said. "He exposed himself today in the sight of the slave girls of his subjects like a vulgar person would expose himself."

²¹ David replied to Michal, "It was before the LORD who chose me over your father and his whole family to appoint me ruler over the LORD's people Israel that I danced. I will dance before the LORD, ²² and I will dishonor myself and humble myself even more. However, by the slave girls you spoke about, I will be honored." ²³ And Saul's daughter Michal had no child to the day of her death.

Good leadership is faithful to God and cares more about what God thinks than what people (even powerful people) think. It's a good reminder that our leadership is a gift of stewardship. First and foremost, we worship and serve God, and in that, we find ourselves helping others fix their attention on Him. If we worship in order to exalt ourselves, we've missed the whole point. So let's worship like David, with humility and great gratitude for who our God is and all He's done.

Psalms of David

Surely the most famous of David's psalms is Psalm 23, which declares his dependance on the Lord, as a sheep with his shepherd, and celebrates the hope and blessing found in Him.

The LORD is my shepherd,
I shall not want.
² He makes me lie down in green pastures;
He leads me beside quiet waters.
³ He restores my soul;
He guides me in the paths of righteousness
For His name's sake.
⁴ Even though I walk through the valley of the shadow of death,
I will fear no evil, for You are with me;
Your rod and Your staff, they comfort me.
⁵ You prepare a table before me in the presence of my enemies;
You have anointed my head with oil and my cup overflows.
⁶ Surely goodness and lovingkindness will follow me all the days of my life,
and I will dwell in the house of the LORD forever.

Another of David's well-known psalms is Psalm 51, written after his sin with Bathsheba, this is a powerful prayer of repentance and his plea for a clean heart.

¹ Have mercy on me, O God,
*   according to your unfailing love;*
according to your great compassion
*   blot out my transgressions.*
² Wash away all my iniquity
*   and cleanse me from my sin.*
³ For I know my transgressions,
*   and my sin is always before me.*
⁴ Against you—you above all—have I sinned
*   and done what is evil in your sight;*
so you are right in your verdict
*   and justified when you judge.*
⁵ Surely, I was sinful at birth,

sinful from the time my mother conceived me.
⁶ Yet you desired faithfulness even in the womb;
*   you taught me wisdom in that secret place.*
⁷ Cleanse me with hyssop, and I will be clean;
*   wash me, and I will be whiter than snow.*
⁸ Let me hear joy and gladness;
*   let the bones you have crushed rejoice.*
⁹ Hide your face from my sins
*   and blot out all my iniquity.*
¹⁰ Create in me a pure heart, O God,
*   and renew a steadfast spirit within me.*
¹¹ Do not cast me from your presence
*   or take your Holy Spirit from me.*
¹² Restore to me the joy of your salvation
*   and grant me a willing spirit, to sustain me.*
¹³ Then I will teach transgressors your ways,
*   so that sinners will turn back to you.*
¹⁴ Deliver me from the guilt of bloodshed, O God,
*   you who are God my Savior,*
*   and my tongue will sing of your righteousness.*
¹⁵ Open my lips, Lord,
*   and my mouth will declare your praise.*
¹⁶ You do not delight in sacrifice, or I would bring it;
*   you do not take pleasure in burnt offerings.*
¹⁷ My sacrifice, O God, is a broken spirit;
*   a broken and contrite heart*
*   you, God, will not despise.*
¹⁸ May it please you to prosper Zion,
*   to build up the walls of Jerusalem.*
¹⁹ Then you will delight in the sacrifices of the righteous,
*   in burnt offerings offered whole;*
*   then bulls will be offered on your altar.*

Psalm 142 is a lament written by David while hiding from Saul, expressing his fear and his trust in God during a time of great distress:

¹ To the LORD I cry out;
to the LORD I plead for mercy.
² I pour out my lament before him;
I tell him about my troubles…

Psalm 27 is a psalm about the security found in God:

¹The LORD is my light and my salvation—
whom shall I fear?
The LORD is the stronghold of my life—
of whom shall I be afraid?...

Psalm 18 is a psalm of thanksgiving and praise for God's deliverance from his enemies and from King Saul:

¹I love you, LORD, my strength.
²The LORD is my rock, my fortress and my deliverer;
my God is my rock, in whom I take refuge,
my shield and the horn of my salvation, my stronghold.
³I called to the LORD, who is worthy of praise,
and I have been saved from my enemies.
⁴The cords of death entangled me;
the torrents of destruction overwhelmed me.
⁵The cords of the grave coiled around me;
the snares of death confronted me.
⁶In my distress I called to the LORD;
I cried to my God for help.
From his temple he heard my voice;
my cry came before him, into his ears...

⁴⁶The LORD lives! Praise be to my Rock!
Exalted be God my Savior!
⁴⁷He is the God who avenges me,
who subdues nations under me,
⁴⁸who saves me from my enemies.
You exalted me above my foes;
from a violent man you rescued me.
⁴⁹Therefore I will praise you, LORD, among the nations;
I will sing the praises of your name.
⁵⁰He gives his king great victories;
he shows unfailing love to his anointed,
to David and to his descendants forever.

Psalms of Asaph

Psalm 73 is one of my favorites as a profound inward struggle that begins with Asaph's envy of the wicked, but ends with a powerful affirmation of faith after entering the sanctuary, leading to the realization that being near to God is the best place to be:

1 Surely God is good to Israel,
*   to those who are pure in heart.*
2 But as for me, my feet had almost slipped;
*   I had nearly lost my foothold.*
3 For I envied the arrogant
*   when I saw the prosperity of the wicked.*
4 They have no struggles;
*   their bodies are healthy and strong.*
5 They are free from common human burdens;
*   they are not plagued by human ills.*
6 Therefore pride is their necklace;
*   they clothe themselves with violence.*
7 From their callous hearts comes iniquity;
*   their evil imaginations have no limits.*
8 They scoff, and speak with malice;
*   with arrogance they threaten oppression.*
9 Their mouths lay claim to heaven,
*   and their tongues take possession of the earth.*
10 Therefore their people turn to them
*   and drink up waters in abundance.*
11 They say, "How would God know?
*   Does the Most High know anything?"*
12 This is what the wicked are like—
*   always free of care, they go on amassing wealth.*
13 Surely in vain I have kept my heart pure
*   and have washed my hands in innocence.*
14 All day long I have been afflicted,
*   and every morning brings new punishments.*
15 If I had spoken out like that,
*   I would have betrayed your children.*
16 When I tried to understand all this,
*   it troubled me deeply*
17 till I entered the sanctuary of God;
*   then I understood their final destiny.*

¹⁸ Surely you place them on slippery ground;
*   you cast them down to ruin.*
¹⁹ How suddenly are they destroyed,
*   completely swept away by terrors!*
²⁰ They are like a dream when one awakes;
*   when you arise, Lord,*
*   you will despise them as fantasies.*
²¹ When my heart was grieved
*   and my spirit embittered,*
²² I was senseless and ignorant;
*   I was a brute beast before you.*
²³ Yet I am always with you;
*   you hold me by my right hand.*
²⁴ You guide me with your counsel,
*   and afterward you will take me into glory.*
²⁵ Whom have I in heaven but you?
*   And earth has nothing I desire besides you.*
²⁶ My flesh and my heart may fail,
*   but God is the strength of my heart*
*   and my portion forever.*
²⁷ Those who are far from you will perish;
*   you destroy all who are unfaithful to you.*
²⁸ But as for me, it is good to be near God.
*   I have made the Sovereign LORD my refuge;*
*   I will tell of all your deeds.*

Psalm 50 is a psalm about the essence of true worship, emphasizing that God desires sincere thankfulness over mere outward rituals:

¹⁰ Every animal of the forest is mine,
The cattle on a thousand hills.
¹¹ I know every bird of the mountains,
And everything that moves in the field is mine.
¹² If I were hungry I would not tell you,
For the world is mine, and everything it contains.
¹³ Shall I eat the flesh of bulls
Or drink the blood of male goats?

Psalms of the Sons of Korah

Psalm 42 is also well-known, expressing a spiritual longing for God in beautiful poetic language:

Psalm 47 declares the true awesomeness of God and calls for celebratory clapping and shouts of praise:

King Hezekiah

In Isaiah 38, King Hezekiah expresses his gratitude to God through a poem in response to His mercy in saving him from a dreadful illness and for defending the city from the Assyrians. The poem closes with a lifelong commitment to public worship together with the congregation of saints, saying:

Music in the New Testament

The Gospels

Matthew 26:30 and Mark 14:26 make mention that Jesus and His disciples went out to the Mount of Olives *after singing a hymn*. Psalm 118 was the final "Hallel" psalm traditionally sung at the end of the Passover celebration during that time, which is why scholars believe it was the hymn Jesus and his disciples likely sang that night. It's a beautiful picture of Christ as the "Light of the World" given to us, and of the salvation that was soon to come through His finished work on the cross. Imagine Jesus and the twelve singing this hymn after He declares to them the New Covenant in His blood. Here's an excerpt:

Give thanks to the LORD, for he is good;
his faithful love endures forever.
I called to the LORD in distress;
the LORD answered me with freedom.

The LORD is my strength and my song;
he has become my salvation.
I will give thanks to you because you have answered me
and have become my salvation.

The stone the builders rejected
has become the cornerstone.
This came from the LORD;
It is wondrous in our sight.

This is the day that the LORD has made;
Let's rejoice and be glad in it.
He who comes in the name of the LORD is blessed.
From the house of the LORD, we bless you.

The LORD is God,
and has given us light.
Give thanks to the LORD, for he is good;
His faithful love endures forever.

Also, in the Gospel of Luke, we see the multitude of angels declaring God's praise when the promised Messiah is born and announced to the people as their Savior:

Luke 2:9-14
9 An angel of the Lord appeared to them, and the glory of the Lord shone around them, and they were terrified. 10 But the angel said to them, "Do not be afraid. I bring you good news that will cause great joy for all the people. 11 Today in the town of David a Savior has been born to you; he is the Messiah, the Lord. 12 This will be a sign to you: You will find a baby wrapped in cloths and lying in a manger."

13 Suddenly a great company of the heavenly host appeared with the angel, praising God and saying,

14 "Glory to God in the highest heaven,
*   and on earth peace to those on whom his favor rests."*

It's unclear whether the angels sing their praise or simply speak it out, but nevertheless, it is a beautiful expression of worship—heralding the coming of Jesus, our Immanuel.

The Book of Acts
Acts 16:25 tells us that while imprisoned in Philippi, Paul and Silas prayed and "sang hymns of praise to God" around midnight. The other prisoners listened as they sang, and their worship was followed by a violent earthquake that shook the prison, opened the doors, unfastened everyone's chains and led to the salvation of the jailer and his whole household.

The Bible doesn't specify the exact psalm that Paul and Silas sang, but many scholars believe they sang from Psalms 113–118, which were known as the "great Hallel" (Hallel means "praise") These psalms were sung during the Passover, expressing reliance on God and offering praise to Him for His faithful love and deliverance:

Psalm 113:1-3
Praise the LORD, you his servants;
Let the name of the LORD be praised,
both now and forevermore.
From the rising of the sun to the place where it sets,
the name of the LORD is to be praised.

Psalm 116:1
I love the LORD, because he has heard my voice and my pleas for mercy.

Psalm 116:2
I will call on him as long as I live.

Psalm 118:6
The LORD is on my side; I will not fear. What can man do to me?

Psalm 118:25
O LORD, save us, we pray...

Others suggest they may have been quoting from Psalm 119, specifically the verses that talk about remembering God's law and giving thanks in the night, or possibly Psalm 146 which gives praise to God in the time of trouble or imprisonment:

Psalm 119:55
In the night, LORD, I remember your name, that I may keep your law.

Psalm 119:61-62
Though the wicked bind me with ropes, I will not forget your law. At midnight I rise to give you thanks for your righteous laws.

Psalm 146:2-7
I will praise the LORD all my life;
*   I will sing praise to my God as long as I live...*
Blessed are those whose help is the God of Jacob,
*   whose hope is in the LORD their God.*
He is the Maker of heaven and earth,
*   the sea, and everything in them—*
*   he remains faithful forever.*
He upholds the cause of the oppressed
*   The LORD sets prisoners free...*

The Epistles

Regarding music in the Epistles, we see instructions to sing with gratitude and build others up through song:

Ephesians 5:19
Sing psalms and hymns and spiritual songs among yourselves, and make music to the Lord in your hearts.

Colossians 3:16
Let the word of Christ dwell in you richly, teaching and admonishing one another in all wisdom, singing psalms and hymns and spiritual songs, with thankfulness in your hearts to God.

James 5:13
Is anyone among you suffering? Let him pray. Is anyone cheerful? Let him sing praise.

The Book of Revelation

In the book of Revelation, we see a vision of heavenly worship centered around God's throne, glory and power, as the four creatures, the 24 elders, the multitudes from every nation, and the 144,000, sing and declare the holiness and victory of our great God and of Christ the Lamb:

Revelation 4:8-11
[8] *Each of the four living creatures had six wings and was covered with eyes all around, even under its wings. Day and night they never stop saying:*

> *"Holy, holy, holy*
> *is the Lord God Almighty,*
> *who was, and is, and is to come."*

[9] *Whenever the living creatures give glory, honor and thanks to him who sits on the throne and who lives for ever and ever,* [10] *the twenty-four elders fall down before him who sits on the throne and worship*

him who lives for ever and ever. They lay their crowns before the throne and say:

¹¹ *"You are worthy, our Lord and God,*
to receive glory and honor and power,
for you created all things,
and by your will they were created
and have their being."

Revelation 5:8-14

⁸ And when he had taken it, the four living creatures and the twenty-four elders fell down before the Lamb. Each one had a harp and they were holding golden bowls full of incense, which are the prayers of God's people. ⁹ And they sang a new song, saying:

"You are worthy to take the scroll
and to open its seals,
because you were slain,
and with your blood you purchased for God
persons from every tribe and language and people and nation.
¹⁰ *You have made them to be a kingdom and priests to serve our God,*
and they will reign on the earth."

¹¹ Then I looked and heard the voice of many angels, numbering thousands upon thousands, and ten thousand times ten thousand. They encircled the throne and the living creatures and the elders. ¹² In a loud voice they were saying:

"Worthy is the Lamb, who was slain,
to receive power and wealth and wisdom and strength
and honor and glory and praise!"

¹³ Then I heard every creature in heaven and on earth and under the earth and on the sea, and all that is in them, saying:

"To him who sits on the throne and to the Lamb
be praise and honor and glory and power,
for ever and ever!"

[^14] The four living creatures said, "Amen," and the elders fell down and worshiped.

Revelation 7:9-12

[^9] After this I looked, and there before me was a great multitude that no one could count, from every nation, tribe, people and language, standing before the throne and before the Lamb. They were wearing white robes and were holding palm branches in their hands. [^10] And they cried out in a loud voice:

"Salvation belongs to our God,
who sits on the throne,
and to the Lamb."

[^11] All the angels were standing around the throne and around the elders and the four living creatures. They fell down on their faces before the throne and worshiped God, [^12] saying:

"Amen!
Praise and glory
and wisdom and thanks and honor
and power and strength
be to our God for ever and ever.
Amen!"

Revelation 14:3

[^3] And they sang a new song before the throne and before the four living creatures and the elders. No one could learn the song except the 144,000 who had been redeemed from the earth.

Revelation 15:1-4

[^1] I saw in heaven another great and marvelous sign: seven angels with the seven last plagues—last, because with them God's wrath is

completed. **²** And I saw what looked like a sea of glass glowing with fire and, standing beside the sea, those who had been victorious over the beast and its image and over the number of its name. They held harps given them by God **³** and sang the song of God's servant Moses and of the Lamb:

"Great and marvelous are your deeds,
Lord God Almighty.
Just and true are your ways,
King of the nations.
***⁴** Who will not fear you, Lord,*
and bring glory to your name?
For you alone are holy.
All nations will come
and worship before you,
for your righteous acts have been revealed."

Revelation 19:1-10
¹ After this I heard what sounded like the roar of a great multitude in heaven shouting:

"Hallelujah!
Salvation and glory and power belong to our God,
***²** for true and just are his judgments.*
He has condemned the great prostitute
who corrupted the earth by her adulteries.
He has avenged on her the blood of his servants."

³ And again they shouted:

"Hallelujah!
The smoke from her goes up for ever and ever."

⁴ The twenty-four elders and the four living creatures fell down and worshiped God, who was seated on the throne. And they cried:

"Amen, Hallelujah!"

⁵ Then a voice came from the throne, saying:

"Praise our God,
all you his servants,
you who fear him,
both great and small!"

⁶ Then I heard what sounded like a great multitude, like the roar of rushing waters and like loud peals of thunder, shouting:

"Hallelujah!
For our Lord God Almighty reigns.
⁷ *Let us rejoice and be glad*
and give him glory!
For the wedding of the Lamb has come,
and his bride has made herself ready.
⁸ *Fine linen, bright and clean,*
was given her to wear."

(Fine linen stands for the righteous acts of God's holy people.)

⁹ Then the angel said to me, "Write this: Blessed are those who are invited to the wedding supper of the Lamb!" And he added, "These are the true words of God."

¹⁰ At this I fell at his feet to worship him. But he said to me, "Don't do that! I am a fellow servant with you and with your brothers and sisters who hold to the testimony of Jesus. Worship God!

In Conclusion

Throughout the prior generations and into the future, music has been and always will be a powerful tool for communication—communication *to* God, *about* God and *for the glory of* God. Both the Old and New Testaments strongly support the use of music in worship. The extensive anthology of actual songs found in the Old Testament and the continual encouragement to sing and make music in the New Testament indicates how incredibly valuable creative musical expression is in the worship of, and communion with, our holy and loving God.

The Bible describes the angels of God and the people of God honoring, praying, celebrating, grieving, heralding and faithfully declaring His character, His coming, and His praises with:

  -Horned Instruments: Trumpets & Pipes
  -Stringed Instruments: Harps & Lyres
  -Percussion: Tambourines, Sistrums, Cymbals & Claps
  -Voices: Melodies, Choirs, and Thunderous, Joyful, Victorious Shouts!

There are no New Testament instructions outlining the type of instruments to be used (or not used), and no particular "style" of music is recommended or forbidden. The simple command is to sing "to God with gratitude in your hearts" (Colossians 3:16).

So may the love of Christ compel us to live a life of worship and may our songs be a true reflection of our love for the One who first loved us.

Reflection & Discussion Questions

1. Using Psalm 105:1–5 as a model, identify where you see the **Five P's** (Power, Praise, Propitiation, Prayer, Purpose) in *one* additional passage from this chapter or in a song you sing at church.

2. Which biblical song from this chapter (Moses and Miriam, Deborah, David, Asaph, Sons of Korah, Hezekiah, the Hallel, Revelation) impacted you or resonated with you the most, and why?

3. Consider David's worship in 2 Samuel 6 and 1 Chronicles 16. Where do you see the balance of *reverence* and *unashamed joy*? How can your team pursue both without drifting into stoicism or spectacle?

4. Compare Psalm 51 (repentance) and Psalm 18 (victory/thanksgiving). What are some song choices you can make to include both *confession* and *celebration* in your worship sets?

5. In Psalm 73, Asaph moves from envy to nearness by entering the sanctuary. How can gathered worship (songs, Scripture, and prayer) shepherd people through honest struggle toward gospel hope?

6. Psalm 50 rebukes empty rituals and calls for *thanksgiving* and *obedience*. What safeguards can your team put in place so musical excellence never replaces spiritual integrity?

Father, thank You for the gift of music and the privilege of praising You. Shape our hearts to worship in Spirit and in truth. Let our songs declare Your power, overflow with praise, point clearly to the cross, rise as sincere prayer, and send us on purpose into Your world. Guard us from empty ritual and self-focus; teach us to honor You with grateful, obedient lives. As we sing Your Word, form Christ in us, strengthen Your church, and draw the lost to Jesus. Make our gatherings a foretaste of heaven—where every tribe and tongue exalts the Lamb who was slain. We offer You our voices, our gifts, and our lives. Use them for Your glory alone. In Jesus' name, amen.

10

WORSHIP IN THE PRACTICAL

Lastly, as we close out this book, I'd like to take some time to consider the very practical elements of worship and ministry. Each church and ministry team should strive to have clear communication and clear expectations so everyone involved can have a sense of structure, along with the tools and training needed to thrive in their role.

Though the specific tools may change over the years, these are some suggested practices that I've found to serve teams well. Let's take a look at them together.

Administration

One of the most important areas we must remember to give attention to is the area of administration. The practical mechanics can make or break your effectiveness in serving the team and therefore can greatly impact the entirety of the church's ministry. For those of us who take on a leadership role, we must view the handling of practical matters as "spiritual acts of worship" (Romans 12:2), and be sure not to neglect the nuts and bolts that keep the car running—or, for those who prefer the more organic—the faithful pruning and gardening that keep the organism alive and flourishing.

Here are some practical areas that you should attend to, to help set yourself and your ministry team up for success:

On-Boarding

Create an on-boarding process that is foolproof so no one ever falls through the cracks. The last thing anyone wants is for people to be dropped or forgotten and cause relational hardship before even beginning the relationship.

If someone emails or approaches you to learn about how to get involved in your ministry, share the process with them so they have a clear picture of what's to be expected and add them into a workflow *immediately* so you don't forget to follow up with them to continue the conversation and on-boarding process. You can also create a ministry application in Planning Center People "Forms" and send them a link to your church's website where they can fill out the ministry application and have it automatically add them into your Planning Center "Workflow".

My Planning Center People "Workflow" has these steps:

1. Reply to Interest
2. Send Link to Ministry Application (or give a physical copy)
3. Ministry Application Received
4. Check References
5. Run Background Check
6. Schedule Meeting & Audition
7. Setup New Team Member in Planning Center Services
8. Schedule to Serve

Auditions

Make your audition process as relaxed as you can while keeping the bar set at the necessary standard for the team and church to be served and stewarded well. In my process, I determine a meeting time that works for us to get together about a week or two in the future and then give the auditionee 3 songs to work on at home. I email them audio files and chord charts and ask them to come prepared to play (or sing) their parts with the band (or with myself and the tracks).

Again, make it a pleasant experience—offer water, coffee or a snack and get to know this brother or sister. Swap brief testimonies and learn about who they are, what they enjoy, and what they value. Then share your heart for the ministry and discuss details about any important team expectations, so they understand the commitment and everything you want them to know up front.

After that, you can run your audition and give them some feedback on what you appreciate, along with what might need tightening up. Let them know you will reconnect in a few days to give them more info and discuss what might be the best way to move forward. Hopefully that's officially joining the team, but in some cases, it can mean directing people to other areas of ministry or helping them develop further so they can re-audition in the future if they aren't quite ready.

In those cases, I encourage you to have some resources available for those who want to grow. You can share those and then suggest that they contact you again when they feel they have made the progress necessary to move forward. If you have names of local instructors and links to training videos or app suggestions for them, it shows that you care and want to see them continue to develop.

Expectations

During your audition time and at your annual team meeting, it's always good to make sure team expectations are clear. If you are the Worship Pastor or Director at your church, you are the one pastoring, serving, leading and stewarding your team and you have the power to set them up for success or make everything difficult for them. Be sure to be organized and communicate well. Serve the people who serve. They are making sacrifices—practicing at home during the week, showing up for rehearsals, run-throughs and often engaging in multiple church services, so be sure to lift the burdens you can lift for them and make it easy for them to have the tools, training and clarity they need to thrive in their role.

Here are some of the expectations I communicate with my teams and ways I strive to set them up for success:

Weekly Schedule

Mondays

Worship sets are prepared by end-of-day on Mondays to give time to practice at home during the week. There are audio files and chord charts available in Planning Center Services in *all* keys to help vocalists find appropriate keys for their voices and to offer capo'd versions for guitarists to select from. Vocalists, please let your team leader know if you need to adjust the key of a song to better fit your vocal range.

Note to Team Leaders: Try to familiarize yourself with the ranges of your lead vocalists so you can build your sets with greater confidence.

Tuesdays & Wednesdays

-Ask for clarity on anything in the set, or anything regarding the weekend, that you have a question about.

-We expect practice to happen at home and each band member to come prepared to Rehearsal.

Thursdays

-We have a mid-week Full Band Rehearsal on Thursday evenings.

-Please be on time. In the rare event that you are going to be late, please let your team leader know.

-At Rehearsal we want to stay focused and respect everyone's time while also keeping things casual so we can encourage relationship and spend a little time in prayer for one another and the church.

-Bring some water, a snack and a good attitude to help the whole team succeed.

Weekends

-On weekends, we expect band members to help setup and teardown their specific area and items on stage and to sit in church for at least one weekend service.

-We ask that band members use discretion in regards to modest attire. We're fine with casual and dressy clothing (just try not to stumble or distract others with gaudy or revealing apparel).

-If you have any questions, please let us know.

-Stay engaged, enjoy the moment, and high-five your team *and the production volunteers* when you're done! Encouragement and comradery are always welcome and beneficial.

Remember to always be prayerful for your team and church, and also in all of the practical elements as well.

Overview
Mon-Wed: Practice at Home & Ask Q's as needed
Thu: Band Rehearsal @ 5:30pm
Sun: Setup @ 7:30am
Sun: Run-Thru @ 8am
Sun: Services @ 9am & 11am

The Commitment

The Worship and Production Teams serve at all weekend services. We ask for an **every-other week commitment for a 3 month period** (this means you are committing to serve approximately 6 weekends over a 12 week period). We have a synced quarterly serving commitment for all our volunteer teams so that spouses and families can serve on the same (or opposite) rotation, as desired. The reason we do this is threefold:

1. To Maintain Consistency & Quality
· Malachi 1 & 2 – God deserves our best
· Psalm 33:3 – We are to serve with skill to honor the Lord
· Psalm 47:7 – We are to serve with skill to honor the Lord

2. To Develop Ministry Ownership
· Eph 4:15-16 –The church reaches spiritual maturity as we serve one another
· Romans 12:1 – Serving is our spiritual and reasonable act of worship
· 1Peter 4:10-11 – We steward and administer God's grace by serving others

3. To Allow for Rest
· Avoid burnout by enjoying every-other weekend without any church responsibilities. You can also invite others to join you and sit in service with you when you don't have to serve on a team every week. It's good to serve and it's also good to have down time.

By taking every-other week *OFF* from serving, it allows you to lay down the burden of responsibility at regular intervals so you can invite friends and family members to church and you can give them your full attention during that time. It also allows for you to take certain weekends to simply sit and soak it all in. You can worship, pray, sing, cry or wrestle with the Word of God, without feeling any pressure to hold it all together and perform any duties. Lastly, it gives you plenty of opportunities to plan and take vacations and take care of the other family, life and ministry things that are on your plate without feeling like you've let God and the church down. (Some people want to serve every week and that's great if they're in a season of life that allows for that, but I don't want anyone to feel like that's a normal expectation). Different stages of life require different amounts of attention to be given to different things. (Before I had kids, I served with different ministries five, six, seven days a week because I could, and it was good, but when you get married and have a kid or two or three, ministry *should* look different—because your family is your *primary* ministry. You have to weigh things out and budget your time appropriately). I want everyone to prayerfully make their decisions and be able to confidently honor God and give the right attention to the ministries they have outside the weekend church gathering.

The nice thing about a quarterly commitment is that no one feels like they're trapped in an endless cycle they'll never be able to break free of. You always have the **option** to ***NOT*** renew your serving commitment, but most people *do*, because they've come to love and value it, but when someone needs a break, they can take a break without any judgment from me.

Also, there's the "ON-CALL" position

If you just can't swing a regular rotation or a 3 month commitment, you can request to be **"on-call"** and fill in when someone calls out sick or can't make it on their scheduled weekend. It's great to have **Backups and Utility Players** who are willing to help in a pinch! There's no shame in the On-Call game. We love it when people serve in that capacity.

Tools & Apps

At the time of this writing, here are some of the current industry standard tools that I use and what I tell new team members while I'm on-boarding them:

Planning Center Services

We use the Planning Center Services app for team scheduling, communication, worship sets, and for storing all our audio files and chord charts for practice. You will be invited to create an account associated with our church. Please take time to familiarize yourself with the desktop and/or mobile version of the Planning Center Services app and let us know if you need any help.

Planning Center Music Stand

Feel free to print and use regular paper charts for your music if that is your preferred method, but if you happen to have a tablet and would like to utilize it for worship charts, you can download the Planning Center Music Stand app to view and edit your worship sets and chord-charts. You can also sync and utilize a Bluetooth page-turner if you want to go hands-free. I personally use the AirTurn DUO 500 because it's so quiet.

MultiTracks

We use click tracks, audio cues, background pads, and also some tracks with percussion, synths and strings during our worship services via MultiTracks.

Many churches use Ableton or other DAWs for this as well. I've found MultiTracks to be the simplest and most user-friendly option for this.

MultiTracks also offers the option for band members to access song stems to practice with at home. If you'd like to hear specific parts on certain songs, please let us know and we'll give you access to that via your personal tablet in connection with our church MultiTracks account.

Worship Artistry

We give access to our team members to a tutorial service called Worship Artistry. If you'd like to watch and learn specific parts on certain songs, please let us know and we'll give you access to that service. You can use the service online via their website: worshipartistry.com or download the Worship Artistry app onto your tablet and sign in using your church account.

IEMs & Monitoring Apps

We use IEMs (In-Ear Monitors). If you don't own your own set, we have some we can give you to keep, just let us know.

Panasonic RP-HJE120-K earbuds are an inexpensive option for volunteers who can't afford high-end custom IEMs. I keep several on-hand to give out to new volunteers and as backups.

We also use (a digital sound console with its specific app) that connects our IEMs to our soundboard—for mixing our own monitors on the weekend and at rehearsals. You can download and utilize the app or just ask our Sound Tech to mix your monitor at the board for you. Either way is appropriate.

Liturgy

Each church has its own liturgy (AKA worship style and order of service). Some churches change their liturgy from season to season, week to week or even from first service to second service. Some keep it the same all the time. Here's what I share with my volunteers about our liturgy:

Our Worship

We believe that God is worthy of all praise, reverence, and love, and that the highest calling of a Christian is to worship Him. Music is a beautiful gift and a powerful tool for expressing our worship to God in response to His holiness and love. Each weekend, we seek to create an atmosphere where the church can meet with God unhindered by distractions, to pursue a deeper relationship with Him through song and prayer. We seek to exalt Him for His greatness, praise Him for His goodness, remember His sacrificial love through the cross, to prayerfully seek His wisdom and grace, that we might know and have His heart in order to honor Him and serve those in our church and community.

As our congregation is a multi-generational one with diverse backgrounds, we seek to serve them with a mainstream contemporary musical style that is palatable for the majority, while also including classic songs and traditional hymns on occasion as well.

Our worship environment is casual, reverent and cautiously charismatic as we seek to engage, honor and enjoy God with our hearts, minds, and spirits.

Here are a few different service-flow options I have used over the years in my churches:

Liturgy 1
Welcome
Song 1
Greet One Another
Announcements
Scripture Reading / Call to Worship *as desired (not forced)*
Song 2
Song 3
Song 4
Prayer
Sermon
1-2 Closing Songs & Communion

Liturgy 2
Welcome
Scripture Reading / Call to Worship *as desired (not forced)*
Song 1
Song 2
Song 3
Song 4
Prayer
Announcements
Sermon
1-2 Closing Songs & Communion

Liturgy 3
Welcome
Scripture Reading / Call to Worship *as desired (not forced)*
Song 1
Song 2
Song 3
Prayer
Announcements
Sermon
2-3 Closing Songs with Communion & Prayer Teams Available

Feedback

Lastly, taking time to recap and debrief with your team after your final service of the weekend can be helpful. Celebrating strong points and making note of weak points for future can benefit individuals as well as the team as a whole. You can talk in person or email feedback—good and bad (with suggested solutions) to your team later that day, if you need to gather your thoughts first.

Example

JOHN (drummer)
That fill going into the bridge on Song 1 was super tight! Nice job! Remember not to rush the click next time we do Song 2.
Maybe you can bump the click up a bit higher in your IEM's so it doesn't get lost in the mix when everything gets loud toward the end of the song.

JANE (vocalist)
Great job leading Song 2! Your pitch and tone sounded so good! Keep dialing in the harms on Song 3. The chorus was good, but the bridge had a couple missed notes. Take a listen to the guides in MultiTracks/WorshipArtistry and see if you can sync with that part. Here's the link: https://www.link.com. Etc...

You can even include yourself in the feedback thread to show that you aren't just critiquing others, but also desiring to improve yourself as well.

In Closing

I've attempted to share some practical ways we can worship the Lord, bless the church and set our teams up for success, but ultimately I encourage you to prayerfully seek the Lord for what will best serve *your specific church and team*, and allow God's Word and His Holy Spirit to inform, guide and empower all that you do as you follow Him in your calling and as you seek to serve: *God, The Church, The Lost, The Team and The Moment.*

As we finish, remember that worship is both work and wonder—a spiritual calling that shows itself in faithful preparation, clear communication, and humble service. The practical rhythms, tools, and expectations in this chapter aren't meant to choke joy; they exist to free your team to minister well, protect one another, and point people clearly to Jesus.

Lead with grace, train with clarity, and care for the people who give their time and gifts. When administration and artistry work together, the team and the church can thrive without distraction or hindrance.

Keep learning, stay teachable, and protect your family and your own soul even as you serve. Trust the Lord to bring fruit from your faithfulness, and encourage your team to walk with the Lord—offering their lives and gifts to Him, and also to *rest*. It's not about lifeless perfection in our execution, but living a life of love, joy and gratitude in response to the One who first loved us.

May the Lord bless your planning, steady your hands in the moment, and use your worship to build up His people and draw the lost to the glory of Christ alone.

Reflection & Discussion Questions

1. How does seeing organization, communication, and planning as "spiritual acts of worship" (Romans 12:1–2) reshape the way you approach the practical side of ministry?

2. Is your current on-boarding and audition process clear and kind? What tweaks might help you hold high standards while still creating an encouraging and safe environment?

3. How can you better steward your weekday preparation so rehearsal and worship services run smoothly?

4. How does the idea of an "every-other-week commitment" help protect your spiritual, emotional, and family health?

5. What additional tools, apps or support would help your team grow in excellence and confidence?

6. Which liturgy or service-flow style do you feel best serves your congregation and why?

7. How comfortable are you with giving and receiving feedback? What makes feedback helpful rather than discouraging?

8. What habits can you cultivate to celebrate wins, encourage one another, and stay united as a team?

Discover new music and worship team resources at:

steadfastworship.org

ABOUT THE AUTHOR

Marquis Ashley has served in full-time worship and pastoral ministry since 2004. He is passionate about small-group discipleship, raising up the next generation of worship musicians, strengthening ministry teams, and supporting church-planting. His deepest desire is to help people know Jesus, develop a biblical worldview, and live a life of worship—loving God, loving others, and making disciples.

Marquis studied biblical theology at Moody Bible Institute and Calvary Chapel Bible College. He has recorded and toured nationally, participated in 15 international mission trips, and continues to stay rooted in the local church. Married since 2003, he and his wife have three wonderful kids who love the Lord and have served with them in worship, production, and kids ministry over the years. Marquis enjoys family walks, songwriting, recording, graphic design, carpentry, strategy board games, WWII movies, anything chocolate-peanut butter, and a good nap.

— • —

"Today's worship leaders are handed big platforms and even bigger spiritual influence— often with little discipleship. Marquis provides a much-needed biblical foundation for authentic worship and practical wisdom for leading God's people in response to His grace and glory. This book will help the next generation grow into mature, effective worship leaders who shepherd the church with depth and integrity."
Scott Cunningham • Pastor | Worship Leader | Founder Likewise School of Worship, Irvine, CA

"I loved it! This book is a fantastic resource for worship teams and any Christian who is curious about worship."
Solo Ray • Producer | Singer | Songwriter | Fresh Life Worship, Kalispell, MT

"A much-needed call back to biblical worship—one rooted in truth, humility, and surrendered lives, not performance or preference. This book thoughtfully shepherds worship leaders and teams toward Christ-centered theology and faithful practice, reminding us that worship is not simply a performance, but a living sacrifice. I'm grateful for a resource that aims at the heart before the stage."
Josh Blevins • Pastor Grace Calvary Chapel, St. Joseph, MO

"I can see Marquis' heart and passion for the Lord in the way he worships and it's inspiring. It drew me in. Thank you Marquis."
Louie Giglio • Founder Passion Movement | Pastor Passion City Church, Atlanta, GA

www.ingramcontent.com/pod-product-compliance
Lightning Source LLC
Chambersburg PA
CBHW071152130726
47998CB00002B/482